EARPS

EMILY STEAD

CLASSIC
FOOTBALL HEROES

EARPS

FROM THE PLAYGROUND
TO THE PITCH

DINO

First published by Dino Books in 2024,
an imprint of Bonnier Books UK,
4th Floor, Victoria House, Bloomsbury Square, London WC1B 4DA
Owned by Bonnier Books,
Sveavägen 56, Stockholm, Sweden

X @UFHbooks
www.heroesfootball.com
www.bonnierbooks.co.uk

Text © Studio Press 2024

Paperback ISBN: 978 1 78946 760 4
E-book ISBN: 978 1 78946 767 3

British Library cataloguing-in-publication data:
A catalogue record for this book is available from the British Library.

Printed and bound in Great Britain by Clays Ltd, Elcograf S.p.A.

3 5 7 9 10 8 6 4 2

For goalkeepers everywhere –
you are the special ones.

CLASSIC
FOOTBALL HEROES

Emily Stead has loved writing for children ever since she was a child herself! Working as a children's writer and editor, she has created books about some of football's biggest stars, teams and tournaments for many a season. She remains a passionate supporter of women's football and Leeds United.

Cover illustration by Dan Leydon.
To learn more about Dan, visit danleydon.com
To purchase his artwork visit etsy.com/shop/footynews
Or just follow him on X @danleydon

TABLE OF CONTENTS

ACKNOWLEDGEMENTS

My first thank you is to Bonnier Books UK for adding me to their squad!

To every teacher, bookseller and librarian who has helped get the books into the hands of readers special thanks are due. And of course, an extra-special mention goes to you, the readers and fans – without you there wouldn't be any Heroes.

I was hugely honoured to be asked to share the story of Mary Earps, a remarkable Lioness whose journey has seen her go from almost walking away from football to becoming the best women's goalkeeper in the whole world. Her heroics on the pitch and mission to make goalkeeping cool have deservedly won her an army of fans, young and old, as well as the inspired nickname Mary, Queen of Stops. Long may her reign continue!

CHAPTER 1

THE GOLDEN GLOVE

20 August 2023, Stadium Australia, Sydney
Women's World Cup Final – Spain vs England

Neither England nor their opponents Spain had ever
reached the final of a Women's World Cup before.
Both teams were desperate to add the little star
reserved for world champions above the crest on their
shirts, a star that would never fade.

The last time the two nations had met was in
Brighton, during the quarter-finals of Euro 2022, when
England had come from behind to earn a memorable
victory in extra time. Many of the Lionesses agreed
that Spain had been their toughest challengers in

the tournament: their squad was packed with clever, technical players who loved to keep the ball. And since the previous summer, they had become even better.

England's goalkeeper Mary Earps had been outstanding that night in Brighton, making crucial saves to keep her team's hopes alive. But without the home advantage in Sydney and with Spain hungry for revenge, a second victory would be far from easy.

The Lionesses started brightly, pressing high up the pitch. Lauren Hemp had an early chance, but saw a curled shot bounce back off the crossbar – a sign perhaps that luck might not be on England's side.

Before long, though, Spain took control of the game, passing the ball in perfect tiki-taka triangles. Mary was forced into making her first big save when Spain starlet Salma Paralluelo flashed the ball across goal, finding England's keeper parrying the rebound.

'COME ON!' Mary screamed at the top of her lungs. She had never been afraid to make herself heard!

Shortly after, Spain were on the attack again. *La Roja* spotted a gaping hole in England's defence with Olga Carmona collecting the ball on the left wing.

With no options in the box, Carmona slashed her shot towards the far post with Mary at full stretch. The strike would have to be inch-perfect to beat the world's best goalkeeper... and it was. The score was 1–0 to Spain.

'We have to stay tighter!' Mary slammed her teammates. She wanted this trophy so badly!

As the first half ended, Spain were dominating all areas of the pitch. England were second best, but there was time to fix that. It was up to their coach Sarina Wiegman to try to change the game.

On came Lauren James and Chloe Kelly for the second half, as England switched formations. The Lionesses worked tirelessly, but Spain were too good, creating chance after chance.

Mary pulled off a super stop after Mariona Caldentey's effort struck her strong right hand before bouncing past the post. Danger averted, but only just.

Then in the sixty-fourth minute, disaster! The ball accidentally touched Keira Walsh's hand in the box.

Mary sucked a deep breath in through her teeth. She knew the way this went by now. A torturous few minutes followed, until VAR and the ref agreed at last.

'Handball by Number 4. Decision is... penalty!' the ref announced through her mic.

Up stepped Jenni Hermoso, Spain's record scorer, as Mary strutted confidently along her goal line.

Hermoso drove her shot low to Mary's left, but the England ace guessed correctly and pounced like a cat, smothering the ball in her arms. SAVE! She wasn't called Mary, Queen of Stops for nothing! She stuck out her tongue defiantly, as the English fans roared.

A grateful pat on the back from captain Millie Bright followed, before the defence quickly reset. England were still a goal behind. Was this the spark that would finally ignite the Lionesses' game? Mary wished with every cell in her body that it was.

But Spain's defence stood steadfast, while wave after wave of red shirts swarmed towards Mary's goal. When a chance fell to Spain's Ona Batlle, Mary stuck out a strong foot. Another huge block! Win or lose this game, England's keeper had been unbelievable!

Spain's attempts to time-waste didn't fool the ref, meanwhile – a massive thirteen minutes of added time were announced. It wasn't all over for England quite yet, but it would take something superhuman to suck the ball into Spain's net. Time ticked on with no luck for the Lionesses until all thirteen minutes had passed. In a last desperate bid to equalise, Mary joined England's attack for a corner.

'Go, PUSH UP!' she urged her teammates.

The ball swung into the six-yard box only to be plucked from the air by the Spanish keeper, who dived and clutched it tightly to her chest. Then the whistle blew. Spain had won the World Cup, fair and square.

Heartbroken, the Lionesses sank to their knees. They had truly believed they would be lifting that trophy, with gold medals around their necks. Instead, they had to settle for silver and watch Spain's brilliant squad of players bask in their glory as world champions.

Mary wasn't prepared for just how much the defeat hurt; her heart suddenly throbbed in her chest. Reaching their first World Cup final was still an incredible achievement, but the Lionesses had come to Australia to win gold, not silver.

'We gave it our all,' captain Millie Bright said, putting an arm around Mary.

Mary said nothing, for once lost for words. England's keeper had played brilliantly – the Player of the Match – but it hadn't been enough. She took off her gloves and wiped away her tears.

As well as a runners-up medal, Mary had another prize to pick up – the Golden Glove trophy, awarded to the tournament's best goalkeeper. Collecting it felt bittersweet.

Mary raised the golden trophy aloft, clapping the English fans for their fantastic support.

'Give us a smile, Mary!' said a voice from among the mob of photographers gathered below the podium.

Mary looked back at them glumly. *If only I could swap this for the World Cup trophy,* she wished. *I'd do it in a heartbeat.*

Sure it was nice to be recognised for her talent and hard work – the goalkeeping at the tournament had been better than ever. Stoppers from Australia to Jamaica to Sweden had pulled off saves that had wowed the world, and Mary's performances had seen her voted Number 1 of all the Number 1s! In time, she would look back on this moment as one of the proudest in her career, but right now, all she felt was pain.

The defeat was a setback, but tough times didn't last forever. Mary was a special player at the top of her game. She would bounce back with her Lionesses, hungrier than ever for their next trophy.

CHAPTER 2

COLT HERO

For Mary Alexandra Earps, it all began in the family's
back garden in West Bridgford, Nottinghamshire.
Mary, her dad, and brother Joel, two years younger,
would chase a football up and down the garden
together each night until it got dark, and they came
inside red-cheeked and happy.

One evening, Mary and Joel teamed up against
Dad in goal. Mary flicked the ball up into the air and
booted it towards her brother. Joel collected the pass
and rolled his shot past Dad.

'Woohoo! Premier League, here I come!' said Joel,
raising his arms in the air.

'Me first,' said Mary confidently. 'That pass

was perfect!'

Joel scoffed. 'Don't be silly… girls can't play in the Premier League!'

He hadn't meant it in a mean or even in a jealous way. It was a fact – no girls in England had grown up to be professional footballers.

Mary smiled and said nothing. Instead, a look of concentration flickered across her face. When Joel next passed to Mary, she trapped it with the inside of her foot before sliding the ball past Dad.

'*Gooooaaaallll!!!*' screamed Mary, sinking to her knees on the muddy lawn.

'Great strike, Mary!' Dad shouted proudly.

Mum stood at the patio doors, her arms folded. It was getting late and both kids would need a bath.

'Did you see that shot, Mum?' asked Mary eagerly.

Mum didn't reply. All she could see was mud. The washing machine was going to have a field day! '*That* ball does not come into *this* house!' she moaned.

Both Mary and Joel were good little footballers, and while Joel had just started playing for a junior side nearby, the club didn't have any girls' teams, so Mary tagged along to her little brother's training.

When Mary was about nine, though, a local dad set up a team just for girls, called West Bridgford Colts. Mary was one of his first signings!

In their first few sessions the girls ran around like headless chickens, all chasing the football. It was chaos! But after some basic training they soon began to pass the ball around neatly. As most of the girls wanted to play up front, desperate to score, everyone took a turn in goal.

Then came the week for Mary to be goalkeeper. All the action was up the other end of the pitch, so Mary spent most of the match cartwheeling around her box.

'Mary!' Dad shouted over from the sidelines. 'Keep your eyes on the game!'

Mary pulled a bored face. 'Pllleeeeeeease can I come out of goal now, Dad?' she moaned. 'I want to be where the ball is.'

Dad sighed. He was used to his daughter being dramatic. 'You have to take your turn,' he said. 'Just like everyone else.'

Mary sighed louder. At least she had a nice shirt to

wear. Bright yellow and shiny, that shirt was the best thing about being the goalie.

Moments later, the play switched. An opponent was running into the box when she was accidentally tripped by a Colts defender. The ref had no choice but to give a penalty!

'At last, I've got something to do!' cheered Mary.

Was she nervous? Not in the slightest. Her eyes narrowed with a flicker of determination. As the penalty kick spun low towards her, she quickly stuck out her right leg to block the ball. SAVE!

The whole team sprinted over to smother Mary in a huge hug.

'Great block!' they cheered.

To Mary's surprise, her save felt as good as if she had scored the winning goal!

'No one else could have saved that!' said Dad. And he was right.

Mary paused for a second. Maybe Dad wasn't so daft, after all? And in that moment, in a muddy field in Bridgford, she knew; she was supposed to play in goal.

Mary put up her hand to go in goal again the

next match, and the one after that, and every match from then on. She loved diving around in the mud stopping shots and was brave in a way that not every child her age was. Besides her fearlessness, she was quick on her feet and so graceful with it. Her coach put it down to Mary doing ballet before she started playing football.

In the end, Mary played for the Colts for three seasons. In those early years, football was as much about fun and friendships as it was about skills and saves, and Mary loved every minute.

Mum would have much preferred Mary to stick to ballet, not least because of how many pairs of trainers her and her brother got through each year.

But the more Mary played the beautiful game, the more she dreamed of becoming a footballer when she grew up.

'Why are you encouraging her?' Mary's mum Julie asked her husband. 'She can't be a professional footballer. I'm worried you're setting her up for disappointment.'

Dad wasn't thinking too far ahead, though. 'Just

look at how happy she is with a ball at her feet and those big gloves on,' he replied.

Julie studied her daughter's beaming face. And after that, she stopped worrying.

CHAPTER 3

GROWING UP

When she wasn't playing football, Mary could be
found at a judo class or swimming lesson, performing
in a dance festival or practising the clarinet or piano.
She was never afraid to try new things, even if she
wasn't a natural – anything that was a challenge, Mary
gladly accepted!

Football was the hobby that stuck, though, and by
the time she was thirteen, she had become a brilliant
young goalkeeper. Whether it was clearing crosses,
blocking shots or tipping a ball over the bar with a
leather fingertip, Mary had it all in her locker!

There was exciting news that year too; for the
first time in Mary's lifetime, the FA Women's Cup

final was set to be played at the City Ground in West Bridgford, the home stadium of Nottingham Forest. The European and league champions Arsenal were set to face London rivals Charlton Athletic. What's more, Mary and some of her Colts teammates had been chosen to be ball girls!

Back then, the cup final was the biggest match of the women's season and the only one where the TV cameras turned up.

'I can't wait to be on telly!' Mary told her mum and dad excitedly.

'We know!' they chimed back. She had been crossing off the days on the calendar for weeks now.

Then at last, the day of the match arrived. The streets around the stadium were bustling with football fans, most kitted out in red-and-white shirts and scarves – the home colours of both Arsenal and Charlton.

'They're expecting almost 25,000 today,' a steward told Mary's dad, as they were parking the car.

Wow! thought Mary. It was like a lightbulb had suddenly flicked on in her head. All those people wanted to come and support women's football. She would give her right glove to star in a match like that one day!

Mary took up her place behind the Arsenal goal. It was a great spot to watch Emma Byrne in action – the Gunners' six-foot keeper stood tall between the sticks.

Arsenal were given an early scare after just two minutes of play when Charlton midfielder Katie Holtham slotted home at the far post, but were level five minutes later, when their ace goalscorer Kelly Smith curled home a twenty-five-yard free kick. Jayne Ludlow scored Arsenal's second after fifteen minutes and added a top-corner screamer just before half-time.

'There was no stopping that one!' Mary cheered excitedly.

Emma Byrne turned around in her goal. 'I'd have given it a go!' she joked.

Mary blushed. She hadn't meant to be that loud!

Another Kelly Smith goal late on in the game wrapped up Arsenal's victory. Winning the cup for the eighth time was a joint record.

After the trophy lift, Mary even got to meet some

of the players, including Arsenal's England midfielders Rachel Yankey and Karen Carney. The Lionesses were more than happy to pose for a photo with Mary.

'Thanks!' said Mary, her cheeks flushed pink. 'You were brilliant out there!'

Karen smiled. 'Do you play football?' she asked Mary.

'I'm a goalkeeper.' Mary didn't hesitate.

But not even Mary's dad could have predicted that his daughter and Karen would share the England dressing room just a few years later!

*

One day, just after Mary's fourteenth birthday, a scout stopped by to watch one of the Colts' matches and was impressed by their young keeper. Her shot-stopping was good and she was quick on her feet too, but it was the way she kept communicating with her defenders, warning them to cut out the dangerous balls or hold their position, that really caught the scout's attention. She seemed wise beyond her years.

Afterwards, the scout invited Mary to come for a proper trial, at Leicester City's Centre of Excellence. Nicknamed the Foxes, their women's team played in the Northern Premier League, while their academy aimed to train up young players until they were good enough to join the seniors. Mary jumped at the chance to try out for Leicester!

A week after the trial, Dad came home from work with a present for Mary.

'Here you go, love.' He smiled, handing his daughter the package. Mary looked surprised. It wasn't her birthday.

'*To our fantastic Fox*' – she read the gift tag aloud. *What?* She ripped open the paper to reveal a pair of glistening white-and-yellow goalie gloves.

'So Leicester want me?' gasped Mary, not quite believing her luck.

Dad nodded proudly. 'Of course they do, silly,' he replied.

She squeezed him tightly in a happy embrace. 'Thanks, Dad!'

Mary's progress at Leicester was rapid. She was

promoted to the women's team after only her first season. The coaches wanted to give their first-choice keeper Leanne Hall some competition and Mary was keen to learn.

Leanne made a huge impression on Mary from their very first session together. She was one of the best role models a young goalkeeper starting out in the game could hope to have. Mary saw how hard Leanne worked in training and learned lots from the way she approached the game. Leanne was serious, but calm, and never minded answering Mary's hundreds of questions. What Mary admired most about Leanne, though, was that like Mary herself, she never stopped striving to be better.

Travelling to Leicester began to prove tricky to juggle alongside Mary's GCSEs at school, so a move closer to home with Nottingham Forest made sense. When Mary's time with the Foxes came to an end, Leanne was sad to lose her little apprentice.

'Mary Earps,' said Leanne at their final training session. 'I'll be sure to remember the name!'

CHAPTER 4

BECOMING A BELLE

Mary was still a schoolgirl when she moved on again, this time to Doncaster Rovers Belles, a club in South Yorkshire that played in England's top league – the brand-new Women's Super League.

It was a club with some really strong players, but not much money, which meant that the Belles' stars were often snapped up by bigger clubs who could pay them more. Wisely, the coaches had decided to focus on youth; they were signing young players with the right blend of natural talent and desire to work hard as part of a team. Mary fitted in perfectly!

Having watched the young keeper in action at Leicester and Forest, Doncaster manager John Buckley was delighted to have Mary on board, but it was only at the end of her first training session with the Belles that John realised the rare gem he had unearthed.

He led his new recruit down the corridor at Balby Carr Community Sports College towards the pitches. As they walked, Mary studied the pictures of famous sports stars on the wall. One in particular caught her eye – a photo of legendary basketball player Michael Jordan with his quote:

'Talent wins games, but teamwork and intelligence win championships.'

Young Mary agreed 100 per cent! It took more than just raw talent to be a good footballer... if you weren't a team player then you wouldn't get very far. Being part of a team was one of the things Mary loved most about football – on a football pitch was always where she had made friends. She couldn't wait to meet her new teammates.

For a women's set-up, the club had fantastic facilities, with a great 3G pitch to train on. The Belles played their home matches at the Keepmoat Stadium complex, with the main 15,000-seater stadium hosting a handful of games each season. Mary knew from experience that many other women's teams weren't as lucky, often stuck with waterlogged pitches, freezing cold showers or sometimes no showers at all.

When they reached the pitch, a familiar voice shouted: 'We know this one!'

A young Millie Bright bounded over to give Mary a hug.

'Welcome to Donny Belles,' greeted another youngster called Bethany England.

Both Millie and Bethany had joined the club two years earlier and knew Mary well from starring for England's youth teams together. The pair loved playing in the red-and-white hooped shirts of the Belles and had already broken into the first team.

'Thanks!' Mary said, with a huge beam on her face.

The training session kicked off and Mary settled straight in. She listened to every instruction the coach gave out, and goofed around with her teammates whenever she got the chance. You would never have guessed it was her first day at the club!

Before long, it was time for some shooting practice.

'Let's go then, Mazza!' said Millie, tossing a ball towards the keeper.

This could be tricky – Millie's right foot was like a cannon, while Beth could pick out any square inch of the goal on request with her pinpoint strikes. Mary, though, handled the drill like a pro, confidently making save after save as the shots rained down on her like giant hailstones.

By the end of the session, the Belles' latest recruit had kept out almost every shot from every angle. 'Is that the best you've got?' she teased her new teammates.

On the sidelines, John's eyes were wide. *This one's got real potential,* he thought to himself. *To have such confidence at the age of eighteen… you can't teach that.*

*

That first session set the standard for Mary's time at Doncaster Belles. Of course she made mistakes, it came with the job, but she was in a good place to develop her skills as a goalkeeper.

At first, she started out with the reserve team, travelling forty miles up the motorway for training and often even further for matches. Most of the £25 fee the club paid for matches was swallowed up straight away by her parents' petrol bill.

Dinner was often packed up to be eaten in the car, while Mary also had to squeeze in important revision for her A-level exams coming up. Trying to write while going around corners was especially tricky!

'Slow down, Dad!' Mary would shout, pens and paper flying everywhere.

'I'll be glad when your exams are over,' her dad replied.

'You and me both!' Mary said with a smile.

Then came the day of Mary's final A-level exam – Chemistry – and school was out at last! Mary had always been a grafter at school, and she was clever with it. University next – if everything went to plan. She was too smart to pin all her hopes and dreams on making a living as a footballer – fourteen matches in a season and £25 for each match was just pocket money. Even the 'professionals' in the league had second jobs to pay the bills.

So Mary and her friends juggled part-time jobs with football that summer. Mary put in shifts in a toy shop and at the local cinema, Millie's spare time was spent working as a fitness instructor and a horse groom, while Beth served up fish-and-chips to hungry customers when she didn't have a ball at her feet. New boots didn't pay for themselves!

Mary had just begun an evening shift at the cinema one Friday when she felt her phone vibrate in her pocket. She quickly snuck out to the lobby and glanced down at the screen. It was her coach John calling. *What was so urgent that it couldn't wait until training?*

'I'm at work, boss,' she whispered. 'What's up?'

'Nothing to worry about,' the gaffer began. 'But what time do you finish your shift?'

It turned out that he needed Mary to make her first-team debut, away to Birmingham City the very next day. If she did well, he told her, he wanted to make Mary the Belles' Number 1 keeper for the rest of the season!

Wow! Mary smiled, doing a hushed happy dance on the spot.

'So see you bright and early?' John asked.

'Yes and yes!' Mary replied excitedly. Now all she had to do was find someone to cover the rest of her shift. She was going to need a good night's sleep!

After her debut for the Belles, Mary didn't look back, with the manager giving her a good run of games in the side. Defeats were sometimes tough to take, but Mary was loving the experience. Every game taught her something new and with each flying save she made, her reputation as a talented young goalkeeper was growing.

CHAPTER 5

A TASTE OF THE CHAMPIONS LEAGUE

With their promising teenage keeper between the sticks, Doncaster finished seventh in the Women's Super League, avoiding relegation, two seasons in a row. Mary was getting plenty of game time, but was that all she needed to become a better player?

When her goalkeeping coach left the Belles, Mary began to think hard about her own future too. If she didn't have proper goalkeeping support, how was she going to keep improving?

So when Birmingham City, a bigger club with better players who wanted to challenge for all the top trophies, said they were interested in signing Mary, she had a big decision to make. Moving to Birmingham would mean that she might not get to play many games, but she could learn from more experienced keepers at the club and keep growing her skills. And not only did Birmingham compete in the Women's Super League, but they had qualified for the Women's Champions League that season. Mary might get to share a pitch with some of Europe's top players!

Another reason to move was that, by now, Mary had started university, studying business at Loughborough. Birmingham was much closer to Loughborough, so it would mean she would spend less time driving up and down motorways when she could be resting.

So should she do it?

If I don't keep moving forwards, I'll be standing still, Mary told herself.

Decision made. Some sad goodbyes to her Doncaster teammates followed, as Mary wished them well for the season ahead. She had arrived at the club while still just a kid – a schoolgirl – and was leaving as a young woman. In her breakthrough seasons, she had been given the opportunity to save shots from some of the best strikers in the country, and had made the Number 1 jersey her own. Mary would always be grateful for her time with the Belles, but adventures with Birmingham awaited her next.

*

Birmingham's first-choice keeper was Becky Spencer. Just a couple of years older than Mary, Becky had made a name for herself playing for England's youth teams. Now she was looking to break into the Lionesses' senior team. And she wasn't the only international player at the club: Karen Carney, Laura Bassett and Jo Potter were England regulars – real Lionesses and brilliant role models! Mary was ready to learn from the best. It would take hard work, but she would roll up her sleeves every day in training and get stuck in!

When the Blues' first Champions League fixtures came around in October, Mary was thrilled to cheer on her teammates from the bench. They saw off a Finnish side first to set up a trip to Russia in the Round of 16 the following month.

Strangely, it was Mary's second trip to Russia
that year, having represented Great Britain there at
the World University Games in the summer, before
joining Birmingham. Team GB had brought back the
gold medal!

The Champions League was even more special
than Mary had imagined. The music, the players, the
trophy. Even the ball they played with was elite! White
with purple stars that joined from tip to tip.

In front of a crowd of just a few hundred people,
goals from Izzy Christiansen and Jo Potter saw
Birmingham easily beat FC Zorky, with Mary proudly
leading the cheers for her teammates.

'Yesssss, girls!' said Mary. She couldn't wait for the
return leg in Birmingham a few days later. 'It's going
to be epic!'

For the home fixture, Birmingham were boosted as
the match would be played at the men's ground. The
pitch at St Andrew's was like a lush green carpet!

More than one thousand noisy fans turned out to
watch the game on a dark November night and were
rewarded with plenty of goals. Zorky led at half-

time, but tired in the second half, with Birmingham storming into a 5–2 lead by the seventy-sixth minute. The Blues were home and dry! Time for a triple substitution…

'Mannion, Wilkinson, Earps, you're going on,' their manager, David Parker told his substitutes.

'What, me? Really?' Mary gasped.

David nodded. 'You've earned it!'

It was unusual to sub a goalkeeper in a match unless they were injured, but Birmingham were 7–2 up over the two legs and in no danger of losing the tie. Now was the perfect time to give his young keeper some important experience.

So before she knew it, Mary was standing on the sidelines, as the subs' board showed Number 21 would replace Number 1. Becky jogged off the pitch and gave Mary a gloved double high-five.

'Enjoy, Mazza!' she said, smiling.

This is it, thought Mary. *My Champions League debut!*

Mary would have loved to have made a wonder-save to impress the manager, but instead she had to make do with a couple of touches of the ball, neither of which were at all flashy. The match ended without either team adding to their score.

'So if I didn't let in a goal, can I count this as a clean sheet?' she asked her goalkeeper coach after the match, half-joking, half-hopeful.

He smiled, glancing up at the scoreboard that read Birmingham City 5, FC Gorky 2. 'Why not!' he replied with a shrug.

A Champions League clean sheet! Not too many twenty-year-olds could claim that! And even if it wasn't officially a clean sheet, it was a special night for Mary.

*

By the time the quarter-finals were due to be played in March 2014, though, Mary wasn't on the bench for Birmingham, nor had she suddenly beaten Becky Spencer to the Number 1 shirt. Ahead of the 2014 WSL season, Mary had moved again, in search of more playing time. Birmingham were keen for her to stay, but the club knew that Mary wasn't happy keeping the bench warm. Another WSL club, Bristol Academy (as Bristol City were known at the time) promised to make Mary their first choice in goal. They could offer Champions League football too, and Mary had jumped at the chance to join them.

CHAPTER 6

THE GOALKEEPERS' UNION

Mary's first involvement with the senior Lionesses had come while she was at Birmingham, when injuries to England's strongest keepers meant that she was next in line for selection.

A second call-up to the squad followed shortly after she moved to Bristol. She was exactly where she wanted to be – training with the best goalkeepers in a first-class environment.

'I'm a sponge,' Mary told her fellow keepers. 'I want to soak up every second of my time with you guys!'

The other England keepers, Rachel Brown-Finnis and Karen Bardsley, had quickly taken Mary under their wing. Even though they were three keepers competing for one spot, the trio stuck together, offering each other advice on how to be at their best and save as many shots as possible. With Brownie and KB (as the other Lionesses called them), Mary was in a goalkeepers' union she had never known before, and she couldn't thank them enough.

'Well, we'll need someone good in goal when we give up our gloves!' Brownie joked.

Mary was a pleasure to teach. Sometimes players came into the squad who believed they were better than they actually were, or who thought they should be handed their first cap straightaway. But not Mary – she was humble, patient and keen to keep learning.

Mary knew she could improve in many ways, but if she kept working hard and believed in herself, she felt sure that the day would come when she would make her England debut.

*

Back at Bristol, life was busy! Mary had had to move away from home for the first time, and she was still

juggling her university studies with football. She
missed her family terribly, but having a base in Bristol
meant that she could focus on being the best footballer,
athlete and teammate she could be. Training took place
during the day for the first time, instead of late at night,
and Bristol had a fantastic goalkeeping coach to help
Mary keep improving her game.

At the club, Mary's technical skills got better
and better – she learned how to make split-second
decisions in games that could mean the difference
between winning and losing, and to choose tactics
that would help her team. If she had a question, she
never felt afraid to ask it, no matter how silly it might
have sounded.

Mary's coach and teammates loved her positivity,
and so did the fans. Her name always got one of the
loudest cheers when it was announced before each
game and Mary would spend longer than any other
player signing autographs and posing for pictures with
young fans after the final whistle. Not so long ago, she
had been one of them!

Mary helped Bristol to finish the season in seventh

place out of eight teams, but the Vixens never looked in danger of being relegated. Playing week-in, week-out again in the Women's Super League was helping her develop into a better player, and even when some of Bristol's results were frustrating, Mary always tried to play with a smile on her face.

As well as the bread and butter of the league, Bristol had qualified for the 2014–15 Champions League. They began by sweeping aside Irish side Raheny United in the Round of 32, before a dream draw against Spanish champions Barcelona in the last sixteen.

'Bristol vs Barça – this is going to be BIG!' Mary beamed when the team heard the news. She wasn't anxious about facing such a historic club in the slightest – opportunities to test herself at the highest level didn't come around too often and she was going to grab this one with both gloves.

Her confidence paid off – a clean sheet for Bristol and an own goal by a Barça player ended the Spanish side's fifty-five-game unbeaten run at home. Amazing!

The second leg at Ashton Gate was an even more memorable night. Vicky Losada put the visitors ahead to level the tie, but Bristol struck back with a late penalty to go through as 2–1 winners. It was a famous win that sent the fans wild! Mary, meanwhile, had kept out challenges from Spanish superstars Jenni Hermoso, Alexia Putellas and Mariona Caldentey.

'We did it! You beauties!!!' the manager Dave Edmondson said in the team huddle.

'I can't believe we just knocked out BARCELONA!' Mary gasped.

Bristol were brought back down to Earth with a bump in the quarter-finals, though, as their European dream came to an end against German side, Frankfurt. Mary was called into action early on, stepping up to save a penalty from German goal-ace Célia Šašić, and playing out of her skin for the first half-hour, but even her heroics couldn't keep Frankfurt out forever. Five goals down by the final whistle, Bristol had been torn apart.

Wow, thought Mary. *Those girls are something else!*

A team made up of players from all over Europe, Frankfurt were organised to perfection. Their tactics were spot-on, and each player knew their role precisely.

A tiny seed had been planted in Mary's mind...
German football was exciting, fast-paced, organised.
I wonder whether I'll ever play in Germany?
she pondered.

The Vixens were playing for pride in the second leg,
but unfortunately found Frankfurt in sparkling form
once again. And although Bristol's 7–0 thrashing was
a game to forget, Mary couldn't help but be impressed
by Frankfurt's style of play. The thought of playing for
a German club sparked her imagination. *One day,
maybe!* For now, though, Bristol was home, and Mary
had a job to do.

Following the highs of the Champions League,
Bristol spent the rest of the WSL 2015 season fighting
a relegation battle. They just didn't have the budget
to compete with rich clubs like Manchester City, who
hammered the Vixens 6–1 to seal a sad relegation to
the second tier.

Desperate to keep playing in the top flight, and keep
her ambitions of playing for England alive, Mary left
the club at the end of the season.

CHAPTER 7

ROYALS SWITCH

Offers from some of the 'big clubs' in the league came in, but none could promise Mary that she would be their Number 1. So instead, she joined Reading, who had just been promoted to the WSL. The club was ambitious, and the players there worked hard for each other. Yes, it would be tricky for Reading's squad to stay in the top league, but Mary never took the easy way out. She wanted to push herself to be the best that she could be, and she couldn't do that if she was sitting on a subs' bench somewhere.

By now, Mary was in the final year of her university course, and Reading to Loughborough was not a short trip. Early starts and a three-hour drive to make her

9 a.m. classes some days left her feeling sleepy, but somehow she always had the energy for football.

In the WSL, wins were hard to come by, but Mary knew that she couldn't control everything. All she could do was to try her best to keep the score down with her sensible shot-stopping and strong positioning. And despite the defeats, Mary kept shining in goal.

'What does KB always say? Only take away the positives,' Mary remembered.

By the end of the season, she had made the WSL Team of the Year. Everyone at the club was so proud of their star keeper!

As soon as it was confirmed that Reading were staying in the WSL, the club offered Mary a good contract. They were desperate to stop a bigger club stealing her away.

'Keep doing what you're doing,' the manager Kelly Chambers praised Mary. 'And you'll go all the way to the top.'

Then at last Mary's studies were over. She graduated with honours from university and loved not having to rush around as much. It felt strange not getting up at the crack of dawn to drive to uni or juggle writing essays. Now she could concentrate on becoming a professional footballer. And not only was Mary great at saving on the pitch, by now she had saved enough money to buy her own little house in Reading. It felt nice to put down some roots after travelling from club to club each season.

England had been keeping a close eye on Mary's progress too and called her up to the senior squad again in June 2017. This time, Mary impressed enough to make her debut!

The Lionesses were 4–0 up in a friendly away to Switzerland when coach Mark Sampson subbed on Mary for KB.

'You've earned this,' Mark told her.

'Thanks, boss!' said Mary, pulling on her gloves.

She didn't have many minutes on the pitch, but Mary made sure to keep England's clean sheet. Hopefully, she had done enough to be picked again.

Mary came close to making England's squad for the Euros that summer, but instead Karen Bardsley, Siobhan Chamberlain and Carly Telford made the cut.

These were experienced keepers that Mary had grown up watching and she had huge respect for all three. While she was a little disappointed to miss out, it only made Mary more determined to keep working hard, learning and improving.

*

Back at Reading, with Mary's safe hands in goal, the team was getting stronger and stronger, but there were still lessons to be learned each season.

Mary was on track to earn her eighth clean sheet that season, away to Sunderland, when the game took a dramatic twist with fifteen minutes to play. With a Sunderland attacker bearing down on goal, Mary charged out of her box to close down the angle. Unfortunately, the attacker shot early and the ball hit Mary on the arm.

'Handball!' the ref declared.

'What?' Mary cried. 'You could see it was accidental!'

The referee disagreed. Instead, he decided that

Mary had denied Sunderland a clear opportunity to score and sent the Reading keeper off. RED CARD!

Mary was devastated. She couldn't believe she had been accused of cheating! That wasn't her style at all.

'Don't worry about it,' said Mary's teammate, Fara Williams. 'That was never your fault.'

'You don't know what you're doing!' the Reading fans sang to the ref.

In the end, Reading kept their clean sheet; their strong team spirit couldn't be broken.

That season more than ever, scouts from other clubs had been watching Mary's matches. There were plenty of clubs following her progress, including German champions Wolfsburg.

'Hands off our keeper!' said her teammates, whenever they spotted a scout in the crowd.

'You can't leave us now,' added Reading's captain, Kirsty Pearce.

Mary brushed it all aside. Her focus was on playing well for her current club. 'Just because scouts turn up, it doesn't mean they'll sign you, you guys know that,' Mary said calmly.

She kept working hard and by the end of the season, Reading had marched up the league table to finish in an impressive fourth place.

Soon after, though, Wolfsburg did offer Mary a contract. Ever since Bristol had been thrashed by Frankfurt in the Champions League, Mary had been excited by the thought of a move to Germany. Now, it could really be happening!

She went home to her parents' house to weigh up the move.

'You've played in the WSL since you were seventeen,' said Dad. 'It could be time for a new challenge.'

Mum had to agree. She wasn't thrilled at the idea of her daughter leaving the country, but Mary had finished her studies and was all grown up now. And not many players turned down a club like Wolfsburg!

So together with her parents, Mary wrote a list of all the positives and negatives:

She wouldn't see her family for weeks at a time ☒
She would be starting from scratch in a new

country and league ☒

She would be the club's second keeper behind Almuth Schult ☒

She didn't know any of the players ☒

...and she couldn't speak a word of German! ☒

But . . .

She would be training with and playing against some of the best in the world ☑

Wolfsburg were German champions and played in the Champions League ☑

Thousands of fans cheered the team on each match ☑

She was sure the experience would make her a better player ☑

It would be a huge adventure! ☑

'Show me where to sign!' Mary said decisively.

CHAPTER 8

A WINNER WITH WOLFSBURG

In Germany, Mary had a lot to get to grips with: the culture and language, a new apartment, even driving on the other side of the road! Wolfsburg, she discovered, was a small city and besides the car factory out of which the football club had grown, there wasn't a whole lot to see. Even so, Mary was excited to begin her German adventure.

About half of her new teammates were German, while players from Denmark, Poland, Norway, Switzerland, Iceland and now England made up the squad. Everyone made Mary feel welcome, and being the confident, friendly type of person that she was, Mary quickly fitted in.

Training was tricky at times, though – it was all
in German! But Mary had been good at languages at
school and tried to piece things together as best she
could. Being a goalkeeper meant she had to learn the
language FAST. She had to be able to organise her
defence, call for the ball and understand the ref in
matches. So Mary learned the basics first: 'Out, come
deep, left, right.'

Almuth Schult was Wolfsburg's best keeper and
Germany's Number 1 too. There was plenty that
Mary could learn from her, even with all Mary's
years of experience playing in England's top league.
She couldn't believe how quickly Almuth could
explode into action to make a save. The German was
so powerful!

'Just incredible!' Mary marvelled, as Almuth tipped
a top-corner curler over the bar.

'But you have good skills too!' Almuth praised her.
'You are amazing with the ball at your feet.'

Almuth was right. One of Mary's strengths was her
distribution – she could perfectly pick out a teammate,
whether they were a couple of metres away or way

up in the opposition half. The coaches saw it too and handed Mary her Wolfsburg debut that September.

Mary couldn't wait for the game to arrive, and was extra excited that her parents would be coming to Germany to attend the game.

With the final score of Hannover 0–11 Wolfsburg, the match couldn't have gone much better! Incredible!

'Those She-Wolves are pretty fierce!' her dad joked, after the match.

'I barely touched the ball!' Mary replied. Not that she was complaining.

Later that season, Mary faced a tougher test. With Almuth out ill, Mary would start in goal against Bayern Munich, who were second behind Wolfsburg in the Frauen-Bundesliga. Whether it was the three important points at stake, or Munich's noisy crowd, Mary was feeling unusually nervous. As she trudged towards her goal before kick-off, her stomach was in knots.

It's just another game, it's just another game, Mary repeated under her breath.

But as the whistle blew, she still couldn't shake off

her nerves. Bayern raced into a three-goal lead, the
third an own goal after a mix-up at the back.

'Stay strong!' her captain Nilla Fischer said kindly.

The second half was better, with the She-Wolves
striking twice to save their blushes, but Bayern bagged
a fourth goal in injury time. Disaster.

Back in the dressing room, Mary felt defeated. She
had been so nervous that she had let in FOUR goals
against the club's biggest title rivals.

'I was *schlecht* out there,' she confessed, her eyes
welling with tears.

'You really weren't *bad*,' said her teammate, Pernille
Harder. 'None of us were at our best today.'

Her friend was right, they won as a team and
lost as a team, and Mary hadn't let anyone down.
The problem was that she set such high standards
for herself that when she fell short, the pain hit her
worse than most.

'We move on,' said the manager Stephan Lerch. 'It
may be three points lost, but there are many more
to be won.'

Stephan didn't blame Mary either, and picked

her again for the very next game. Wolfsburg put the Bayern loss behind them, bouncing back with a 6–0 victory and a clean sheet for Mary. That was more like it!

The super She-Wolves went on to finish the season as double winners – claiming the league title ahead of Bayern, as well as the German cup. It was Mary's first taste of silverware – two trophies for all her hard work over the years. Her Wolfsburg move had been well worth it!

*

Meanwhile, the Wolfsburg manager was not the only coach Mary needed to impress; Phil Neville had taken over as England boss, and had the job of forming a squad of strong Lionesses to take the World Cup in France the following year.

Earlier that season, Phil had given Mary her first England start, in a World Cup qualifier against Kazakhstan, a match the Lionesses had won 6–0. A photo of Mary beaming proudly after the match said it all.

'It looks like you've been given the keys to a sweet factory!' Mary's dad said.

'Your smile's not changed since you were little!' Mum agreed.

Mary smiled again. She had achieved the next step on her football journey, but there was still work to be done if she was to make the World Cup squad. It would be a dream to play for the mighty Lionesses in a proper tournament! The twenty-three most talented players in the country would be on the plane to France and Mary was desperate to earn her ticket. Now she had to stay fit and focused.

CHAPTER 9

SQUAD GOALS

Mary's chances of a place in the Lionesses' World Cup squad were boosted when Phil Neville picked her for the SheBelieves Cup in the spring of 2019. England went unbeaten in the mini tournament against three top teams – United States, Japan and Brazil – in America to win the trophy! And while Mary didn't make it on to the pitch, she would head back to Germany with a shiny medal and some special memories.

As for the World Cup squad, Mary was taking nothing for granted.

'You're a brilliant keeper, don't worry,' her Lionesses teammates encouraged her.

'I'm not going to lie, I'll be gutted if I'm left out,' Mary confessed.

She felt like she had come on leaps and bounds since joining Wolfsburg and hoped the coaches could see that too. Playing abroad though made it harder for Phil to watch Mary in action. Had he been watching the videos her club had been sending? She had made some saves that defied gravity in those reels! Fingers crossed.

So when it was revealed that Mary was England's third keeper in the squad, behind Karen Bardsley and Carly Telford, she couldn't have been happier. When Mary broke the news to her parents, her heart was bursting with pride.

'I probably won't get on the pitch, but never say never!' Mary said hopefully.

'NEVER say never!' her dad agreed.

Mary smiled. That was the magic of football – something could happen in an instant and change everything – usually when you least expected it.

*

June 2019, Nice, France

The sunny south of France made the perfect base for England to prepare for the tournament. Training sessions were fun and relaxed, but every player worked her socks off. The goalkeepers were expected to join in all the drills so that they were as comfortable with the ball at their feet as they were diving around on the grass.

Mary loved the rondos best, a drill where two or three players in the centre tried to win back the ball from a bigger team spread out in a circle. Nutmegging the piggies in the middle never got old!

'Gotcha!' Mary teased Beth Mead.

'No fair,' Beth moaned. 'Goalkeepers shouldn't be able to do that!'

It was a squad bursting with talent and the Lionesses' team spirit was getting stronger by the day too. Every player had something different to offer.

Whether it was…

Team captain Steph Houghton's experience,

Jill Scott's boundless energy,
Lucy Bronze's marauding runs up the pitch
Or Ellen White's knack for sniffing out a goal . . .

. . . these Lionesses were fearless!

'Strength in depth' the TV pundits called it, which meant that for every position, there were at least a couple of talented players who could slot into the team. England were full of ambition and had come to France to WIN.

Their start to the competition was pretty much perfect, earning maximum points from their Group D matches. Only Scotland managed to score against them, with the Lionesses claiming clean sheets in their victories over Japan and Argentina. In goal, KB was looking strong.

In the Round of 16, England drew Cameroon, the lowest-ranked team left in the tournament. The result went England's way as expected, but the 3–0 scoreline only told half the story.

Steph struck home a free kick before Ellen added a second. At first the ref had ruled out Ellen's goal, before

VAR decided it should stand. The Cameroon players were so distraught, they refused to kick off again at first! Later, when VAR decided a strike for Cameroon *was* offside, the game came close to spiralling out of control. More tears and tantrums followed.

Wow, Mary gasped from the bench. She might have understood if this were an Under-10s gala, but this was the WORLD CUP! She could barely believe what she was seeing.

Then at last the final whistle blew. The Lionesses couldn't get down the tunnel quick enough.

*

After the Cameroon chaos, the Lionesses needed to let off some steam before their quarter-final. And what better way to do that than to hit the beach! Just across from the team's latest hotel in Deauville, northern France, was a golden sandy beach. The training session that day was focused firmly on fun.

Sunscreen sorted, it was time to let the games begin! Half the Lionesses were handed foam-dart blasters while the other half were given plastic cups in which to catch the squishy bullets.

Mary closed one eye and squeezed her trigger, arrowing a dart towards defender Rachel Daly, who flung out her cup. CATCH!

'Nice shooting, Tex!' said Rachel, faking a Wild West accent. She did play her club football in America, after all.

Next up was Twister. This time Mary played referee, keen to give others a chance to make themselves look silly. Jill Scott accepted the challenge, taking on Leah Williamson, the youngest Lioness.

'Watch and learn,' said Jill, rubbing her hands together with glee. 'WATCH AND LEARN!'

Mary spun the spinner and read out the commands, as a crowd quickly decided whether they were Team Jill or Team Leah. Before long, arms and legs began to tangle.

'Right arm, yellow,' Mary called out next.

It looked impossible for Jill to reach her arm past Leah's left leg, but somehow she did it. Leah had no chance when 'left hand, blue' was her next instruction and she collapsed in a heap of giggles on the sand. Jill was the winner!

'These elastic limbs do come in *handy*, you know,' said Jill, stretching her arms around Mary.

The rest of the Lionesses groaned.

'That's probably enough Twister for one day,' Phil said, gathering up the plastic sheet. 'We don't want any injuries before Thursday!'

That's right! Mary suddenly remembered. Just two more sleeps and England would face Norway at the Stade Océane in Le Havre. Now only eight teams remained in the race to become world champions.

It would be so easy to get carried away, imagining your team raising the shiny trophy aloft, but England couldn't lose sight of the game in front of them. And Norway were the strongest team they had faced in France so far.

'Norway are good, but they're no Lionesses!' her dad told Mary on the phone. He always had some wise words to keep his daughter grounded and Mary's homesickness at bay too.

'Thanks, Dad,' said Mary. 'We'll find a way to win!'

CHAPTER 10

ENGLAND'S EXIT

The next day, after breakfast, Mary's phone began to buzz again. This time, it was her agent Christina with some unexpected news. Mary found somewhere private to talk.

'Sorry about the terrible timing,' Christina began, 'but Manchester United have called. Their keeper Siobhan Chamberlain is expecting a baby and Casey wants to bring you in for next season.'

Manchester United were a huge club in the men's game, but had only recently reformed their women's side. The 2019–20 season would be their first in the WSL, after winning promotion from the Women's Championship. United's head coach was former

Lionesses captain Casey Stoney, who Mary knew well from some of her first England camps. It could be a brilliant move on paper!

But what about Wolfsburg? Was Mary ready to move after only one season? She would likely end up warming the bench for another year if she stayed – Almuth was locked in as Number 1. If Mary did leave, she would be returning to the WSL as the winner of two trophies and the creator of some amazing memories.

Mary told no one about the phone call, not even her England roommate Toni Duggan. If she was going to switch clubs, it would have to wait until after the tournament – there could be no distractions while on World Cup duty.

*

Dad was right about the quarter-final – the Lionesses roared to victory over Norway! First-half goals from Jill and Ellen before a sensational volley from Lucy – the pick of the tournament so far – sealed a semi-final place for England.

Next up, though, were the United States – three-time winners and the reigning champions. England would have to play out of their skins if they were to win, and they would have to do it without their first-choice goalkeeper. In the Norway match, Karen Bardsley had felt her hamstring ping, but had carried on playing until full time. It was only afterwards that the injury was revealed to be more serious than she had thought. KB was still named on the bench for the USA match, with Carly Telford starting in goal, but Phil told Mary to be ready in case of emergency.

'I will be,' said Mary confidently.

The match kicked off and Carly made a strong save early on, but there was nothing she could have done to stop a brilliant header from Christen Press soon after.

'No keeper was saving that,' Mary moaned on the bench.

Just minutes later, though, Beth delivered a dangerous ball to Ellen on the edge of the six-yard box. Ellen, who had already scored five times in the tournament, buried her shot in the back of the net. *Goooooooaaaaaaalllll!*

Mary leapt from her seat and punched the air. 'COME ON!' she screamed happily.

The Americans, though, were not giving up, and at the half-hour mark had scored again – Alex Morgan with another strong header.

Next, Ellen thought she had made it 2–2 with her second cool finish, but VAR ruled England's equaliser offside by a toe. And when Steph missed a penalty and Millie Bright was sent off late in the game, it became clear there was no coming back for the Lionesses. Heartbreak!

Their World Cup was over. Mary and the team clapped the thousands of England fans in the stands for their support through teary eyes. Every player had given her all over the tournament, from the starting eleven to the subs on the bench. To have come so close to reaching the final and leave with nothing was not a feeling the Lionesses wanted to suffer again.

'We'll come back stronger,' Mary resolved.

*

Landing back in England, everything felt strange. Suddenly the faces that Mary had hung out with for the past few weeks, her friends, were no longer there. Those first few days back home with her family, she barely knew what day it was. And she still had to decide where to play her club football next season.

'My head's all over the place,' she told her mum.

'Take your time,' Julie replied. Of course she wanted her daughter to come home to England, but knew that Mary had to make up her own mind. She had been fiercely independent even as a little girl.

In the end, it didn't take long to come to a decision; a week after the World Cup final – which the United States went on to win – Mary signed for Manchester United.

'Something special is happening at this club and I'm excited to become a part of it. It's the perfect place for me to reach the next level in my career,' Mary told the press.

She couldn't have been more right!

Mary's phone exploded with messages from her England teammates, all congratulating her on her return to the WSL.

'You kept that quiet!' Toni Duggan texted.

'I'm sorry, I had to!' Mary replied. Luckily, Toni forgave her.

And although Mary's feet had barely touched the ground since the World Cup, she was already excited for the new 2019–20 season ahead.

CHAPTER 11

BACK IN THE WSL

Casey Stoney's Manchester United team were still finding their feet as they kicked off their first Women's Super League season, with Mary just one of the new faces that went straight into the side. The Red Devils pushed Manchester City and Arsenal all the way in their opening two games and were unlucky to come away without any points.

Despite the losses, Mary was focused on the bigger picture. There were plenty of matches to come where they could pick up points and climb the table. They had looked strong in defence, with Mary the top performer, while the attackers had created plenty of chances. Now all they had to do was start scoring.

'You belong at this level, you've got to start believing it,' Casey told her team in training.

The coach's confidence spread quickly to her players, and in October, Katie Zelem and Jess Sigsworth earned Manchester United a stunning victory over neighbours City in the league cup. The home crowd at Leigh Sports Village was always loud, but this match felt like the team had a twelfth player!

'Revenge is sweet!' said Mary. And a clean sheet made it all the sweeter.

Two more wins followed, with Mary keeping clean sheets both games, before the break for international matches. The club's new keeper was fast becoming a fan favourite. The first time she heard the fans sing her name gave Mary goosebumps!

'We love you Mary, we do,
We love you Mary, we do,
We love you Mary, we do,
Oh, Mary, WE LOVE YOU!'

Wow! It was usually goal*scorers* not goal*keepers*

who got all the attention. Mary puffed out her chest with pride.

After each match, Mary made sure to sign as many flags and pose for as many selfies as she could. Inspiring young girls and boys to follow their dreams was one of her favourite things about being a footballer. Watching the face of a young goalkeeper light up when Mary passed on a pair of her gloves was the best feeling ever!

'Keep working hard and maybe I'll see you on this pitch one day,' she told them.

It was early days in Manchester, but Mary was happy. The fans were fantastic, she loved her teammates, and her coach was helping Mary to really believe in herself. After moving from club to club most seasons, she hoped she could stay at United for a long time.

*

Since the World Cup, the Lionesses had played a few friendlies, with some disappointing results. KB was still

out with the injury that had ended her World Cup,
so Carly had deputised in goal. Then against Brazil,
Mary's chance to shine came at last. Not third choice,
nor second choice… this time Mary was starting
for England!

There was a buzz in the air at Middlesbrough's
Riverside Stadium for the Lionesses' first home match
since the World Cup. England had looked lively in
the first half – even if that had ended goalless – but
suffered a blow soon after the break.

Dazzling forward Debinha got on the end of a Brazil
cross and planted her header goalwards. Mary dived a
fraction of a second too late and felt the ball roll under
her body and across the line. Her heart plummeted.

'Unlucky,' said Steph, picking the ball out of the net.

'I should have done better,' said Mary, furious at
her mistake.

Debinha was on the double a little later, when
her strike from close range took a deflection off Lucy
Bronze. Mary, helpless to stop it, could only watch the
ball loop over her head.

Where was the defence? There was no way that

cross should have been allowed! Mary felt even more miserable. She hated letting in goals.

A late header from Bethany England pulled a goal back for the Lionesses, but it wasn't enough – England had lost. Sloppy errors and missed chances up front had cost them the draw.

'Sorry boss,' Mary apologised after the match. 'It won't happen again.'

If there is a next time, she thought.

Phil gave her a hug. 'It wasn't our night tonight.'

Ellie Roebuck was trusted with being in goal for England's next match, but on a rainy night in November, Mary was back between the sticks for a huge friendly against European rivals Germany. At Wembley Stadium, no less! Only once before had the Lionesses played at Wembley, when they had lost to the same opposition a few years earlier. Mary was playing in the Under-23s back then.

Women's football had changed so much since that game. The Lionesses' performances at the World Cup had made fans fall in love with the team, and now, in 2019, more than 77,000 of them had turned

out to watch their heroes – a record crowd for a
Lionesses match!

Despite being ranked second in the world, Germany
had exited the World Cup at the quarter-final stage,
leaving their fans frustrated. Now, they needed a good
performance as much as England did.

In the tunnel, the two teams stood side by side,
waiting for their cue. They could already feel the buzz
of excitement that fizzed around the packed stadium.

Mary's eyes flicked across to Germany's spectacular
striker Alex Popp. She knew the damage Popp could
do from their time together at Wolfsburg. It was going
to be tough to keep her quiet for ninety minutes.

Stay focused, stay focused, Mary muttered
to herself.

'Ready?' said Phil, patting her on the back.

'Ready,' Mary confirmed.

Mary was right; it was Popp who came closest to
opening the scoring. Lena Oberdorf slid a ball in to
her captain, who struck her shot with force. Mary had
stayed alert and made the faintest of touches to tip it
onto the crossbar and over. *SAVE!*

There was no stopping Popp the next time Germany attacked though – when the striker stooped to meet a cross, a diving Mary could do nothing about her header. *GOAL!*

'Let's settle down, guys!' came skipper Steph's orders.

England battled back and earned a spot-kick next, after German keeper Merle Frohms brought down Ellen in the box, only to see Nikita Parris shoot the penalty straight at the keeper.

An easy stop, moaned Mary.

Ellen wasn't giving up though – the fans had come here to be entertained! On the stroke of half-time, she levelled the score. With more than a hint of offside about her goal, luckily for the Lionesses, the flag stayed down.

After the hour mark, Germany thought they had scored again when Mary spilled a shot straight into the path of Lina Magull for a tap-in. Mary breathed a mighty sigh of relief as the goal *was* given offside this time.

With ninety minutes on the clock, it looked like it

would be honours even, but then came the killer blow. Teenager Klara Bühl broke through England's dodgy defence, before flashing her shot across Mary's goal and into the bottom corner. *2–1!* Germany had done it – they had won the match in added time!

Mary was devastated. She wasn't at fault for the goal, but she had still been beaten. Doubt was beginning to creep into her game. If she wanted to be England's Number 1, Mary knew she would have to train even harder.

CHAPTER 12

ROCK BOTTOM

In February 2020, just before the next international squads were due to be announced, Phil phoned Mary for a quick chat. Although Mary had been playing well for her club, Phil had decided to 'go in a different direction' for the SheBelieves Cup and give some young keepers a game.

'It doesn't mean that you're not in my plans anymore,' he promised.

Fair enough, thought Mary. It didn't feel good, but she accepted the coach's decision with good grace. No player had an automatic right to be in every squad, she knew that. All Mary could do now was to focus on playing well for her club and hope to be picked for the

Lionesses next time.

The tournament came and went with England's defence of the trophy ending in disappointment. The fans began to grumble over Phil's team selections. Then followed events that no one could have predicted: the world went into lockdown due to the COVID-19 pandemic. The Women's Super League was suspended and eventually cut short, with people's health put first.

The players were forced to train at home alone, which was doubly difficult for goalkeepers. But with the help of a rebounder net, weights and a skipping rope, Mary kept fit and tried as best she could to stay positive.

By September the WSL was back at last, for the start of a new season. Mary was thrilled to be back on the grass at Leigh Sports Village, and even though only small crowds were allowed to gather in stadiums, the fans gave the team a real boost.

If United's first match – a draw with champions Chelsea – was anything to go by, it was going to be a strong season for the Red Devils. Mary had made a

string of saves from Chelsea's superstars to help her
team earn an important point.

The following evening she was happily scrolling on
her phone, with her dinner in the oven, when there it
was: the Lionesses squad for their upcoming friendlies
against Germany and Norway. A huge squad of thirty
players would meet up for camp at St George's Park.

Mary's eyes flicked straight to the goalkeepers'
section, only to discover her name was not among
them. The list read: Hannah Hampton (Birmingham
City), Sandy MacIver (Everton), Ellie Roebuck
(Manchester City) and Carly Telford (Chelsea). And
not even a phone call from Phil this time.

The news hit Mary like a train and she dropped to
the floor suddenly, sobbing huge, ugly tears. What had
she done wrong? Was she really not good enough to
play for England anymore?

She lay there for a little while until she eventually
caught her breath. Then she reached for her
phone again.

'Mum, can you come over?' she cried tearfully.

'We're on our way, love,' Julie replied, without a

moment's hesitation.

In the days that followed, there were more tears and a lot of talks with Mum and Dad. Mary had loved football since she was little, but now she wasn't sure if she wanted to carry on playing. Everything that used to make sense in her life suddenly didn't anymore.

'That's it, I'm done with football,' she told her parents. She had reached rock bottom.

'Whatever you decide, we'll be right behind you,' her parents reassured her.

Luckily, Mary did at least feel strong enough to go back to training at Manchester United. She bumped into the men's keeper, David de Gea, at their Carrington training ground. They always stopped to chat when they could – the goalkeepers' union was strong! He asked how things were going.

With no one else around, Mary decided to confide in him. She would usually only share something this big with her parents, but she thought it might help to talk to another keeper.

'Look, I'm thinking about retiring,' she said frankly.

'What? You're younger than me, you can't retire

yet!' David joked.

But he saw a solemn expression in her face he did not recognise, and so took a different tack. So what if she wasn't in the England squad just now? he told her. It didn't mean that she couldn't win back her place.

'Give it until the end of the season, at least,' he tried to persuade her. 'You're at a great club, Casey thinks you're fantastic and the fans adore you. Are you really ready to give all that up?'

Just like Mary, David had had wobbles in his career. Whenever they happened, he tried to focus on the good things in life and think about the joy that football gave him. 'Play like you're a kid again!' he said encouragingly.

So while the England squad met up for camp at St George's Park, Mary took some time to think about things quietly. It was the biggest decision of her life and one that couldn't be rushed.

She played back the conversation with David in her head and had plenty more pep talks from her family. Then at last she reached a decision – she would play on. Of course, the time would come when it felt right to give up her gloves, but that time wasn't now.

In the end, both Lionesses' matches were cancelled amid COVID-19 restrictions, and Phil Neville had managed his last match.

Perhaps the next coach, Hege Riise would recognise what Mary could offer England? The Norwegian was set to take temporary charge of the team, as new boss Sarina Wiegman couldn't yet come in, because she had to take her Netherlands side to the delayed Tokyo Olympics that summer.

Sadly for Mary, a recall under Riise wasn't to be. She would miss out on England's spring friendlies as well as Team GB's squad for the Olympics.

This time, however, Mary took events in her stride. The dark cloud that had hung over her a few months earlier was beginning to lift. She was enjoying her football at Manchester United again and keeping plenty of clean sheets. Whatever the future held, Mary felt a little brighter.

CHAPTER 13

SARINA THE SAVIOUR

The 2021–22 season came with fresh challenges. Casey, the coach who had brought Mary back to the WSL, had moved on from Manchester United, and many of the players were anxious to impress under new boss Marc Skinner. Mary, though, was confident of keeping her place in goal. She had rescued her team on many occasions the previous season, making some sensational saves to help the Red Devils finish fourth.

No one's taking my shirt! she resolved.

Soon after the league had begun, squads for the next internationals were due to be announced. By now, Sarina was in charge, but after being out in the cold with England for almost two years by now, Mary wasn't getting her hopes up for a recall. She was just about to make a glamorous trip to buy some new curtain poles when the email came through – MARY WAS BACK IN THE ENGLAND SQUAD!

'That's brilliant news!' her parents gasped. After everything they had been through together, they felt prouder of their daughter than ever. 'Go and enjoy yourself, love!'

'I will!' Mary promised.

Her next phone call was to her goalkeeping coach at United, Ian Wilcock. She stumbled just trying to get her sentences out.

'Well, that's the first time I've heard you lost for words!' he remarked.

Ian was right, Mary was gobsmacked at the news!

*

St George's Park, Derbyshire, 13 September 2021

Thankfully, Mary only had a few days to wait until the start of camp – she might have burst with excitement otherwise!

It felt incredible to be part of the squad again in what was a fresh start for all the players. England's big names like Ellen White and Steph Houghton were included, as well as a host of younger players, looking to earn their first senior caps. Mary was thrilled that her Manchester United teammates Lucy Staniforth, Ella Toone and Katie Zelem had all made the cut too.

Training was fun, but it was clear from the start that new boss Sarina demanded high standards of her players. Mary was pleased with how she had performed in the sessions – whether it was organising her defenders, making acrobatic saves or generously offering tips to the squad's younger keepers, it was safe to say that all her thoughts of giving up football had been relegated for good. Her positivity and willingness to work hard had not gone unnoticed by the coaches.

On the last day of camp, Sarina's assistant, Arjen, came to find Mary in the gym. 'Sarina would like to see you now,' he said.

Eek! Here we go!

Mary nervously followed Arjen to a plush meeting

room where Sarina was waiting, before Arjen slipped out of the room.

'Hi Mary, thanks for coming,' Sarina said, gesturing to one of those leather bucket chairs you can't help but slide around on. 'Please sit.'

Sarina began by asking Mary how she thought the camp had gone. Had she enjoyed herself? Had she been glad to be back with the Lionesses?

From out of nowhere, tears suddenly pricked Mary's eyes and her pulse began to quicken. *Agh, not now!* She wished she could summon that spell from Harry Potter to make her tears evaporate. How did it go again?

'Being back with the girls has meant more than I ever thought,' Mary blurted out.

'I've missed playing for England so much!'

'That's good!' Sarina said calmly.

Mary studied the coach's eyes. Encouraging. Kind. She took a deep breath and smiled at last. *OK, hit me with it.* She was ready for whatever feedback Sarina was about to deliver. But she needn't have worried – the news was good!

'Look, for now, I see you as my best goalkeeper,' Sarina said plainly. 'But when the injured players come back, I'm going look at everybody the same – I'm going to give everybody a fair chance.'

After feeling like she had been invisible for so long, it was the best news that Mary had had in years! Yes, her place wasn't guaranteed, but she couldn't have asked for anything more. All Mary had ever wanted was a chance, and in return she would give her all.

She thanked Sarina and exited the room. Arjen was waiting outside with Beth Mead, another talented player who had lost her place in the side. Beth looked pale, as though she had been summoned to the headteacher's office, so Mary gave her a smile and a wink.

'Good luck!' she mouthed. 'You've got this!'

*

So the next day, Mary started as Number 1 in Sarina's first game, an important World Cup qualifier against North Macedonia. She didn't see much action as

England ran out 8–0 winners at St Mary's, but she still loved every minute. The Lionesses were more brutal still in their next match a few days later, this time putting ten past Luxembourg.

Sarina's first six matches in charge couldn't have gone much better. In a dream start for the Dutch coach, England had:

Played six.

Won six.

Scored fifty-three goals!

Conceded zero goals!

Six victories and six clean sheets! Mary had at times been a spectator in goal, but had played every minute of every game, her longest run in goal for the Lionesses so far. She could hardly believe her luck. Since that first meeting with Sarina, it was like Mary's world had done a double, no triple, backflip. She felt giddy every time she stopped to think about it.

CHAPTER 14

PLAYING FOR KEEPS

After all the ups and downs that had come before, Mary wasn't about to take her place in the England side for granted. Experienced keepers like KB and Carly were yet to shake off their injuries, while Ellie and Hannah were ready to push Mary all the way too. The year ahead was a huge one for the Lionesses – with a home Euros to host at last in summer 2022 and before that a new tournament, the Arnold Clark Cup. Mary couldn't help but feel excited.

Back at United, she worked like a woman on a mission, ironing out the tiny errors in her game that could lead to a goal. She looked more at ease with the ball at her feet, and organised her defence smartly, while she was fast becoming one of the best shot-stoppers around.

When the players reported for duty at the Arnold Clark Cup, Sarina gathered the goalkeepers to share her plans for the tournament. As it was a friendly competition, she wanted to give as many players as possible the chance to play.

'Mary will play the first match against Canada, Hannah will be keeper against Spain and Ellie will face Germany in our final match,' Sarina explained.

So their opponents were the Olympic champions, the Euros favourites and the two-time world champions. None of the games were going to be easy!

England opened the scoring against Canada, but it was neither Ellen nor Alessia Russo who found the back of the net. Instead, centre-back Millie Bright smashed home a stunning volley from the edge of the area. Millie's days as a striker at Doncaster had served her well!

'What a finish!' gasped Mary.

Canada equalised against the run of play in the second half, though, as Janine Beckie cut inside two

England defenders and let fly with a top-corner curler. Unstoppable!

'We can't back off them like that!' Mary fumed at her defence. One chance was all it took for a top side like Canada to get back into the game.

Hannah kept a clean sheet in a stalemate against Spain next, while Germany's Lina Magull was the only scorer against Ellie in England's 3–1 win. The goalkeepers' union had helped England remain unbeaten and win their first trophy under Sarina! It wasn't exactly the Euros, but winning any silverware felt special to Mary.

*

Thanks to their good performances at the Arnold Clark Cup, Sarina did indeed choose Mary, Ellie and Hannah for her Euros squad. And there was big news for one keeper in particular. Sarina called Mary as soon as she had made her decision.

'I want you to be my goalkeeper this tournament,' Sarina began. 'You are the best we have.'

'I won't let you down!' Mary said, slightly stunned.

'Of course you won't!' Sarina replied matter-of-factly. She had every faith in Mary.

It felt incredible that Sarina trusted her so much.

The tournament arrived at last, after being put on hold due to the COVID-19 pandemic for a whole year. Wembley Stadium had played host to the men's Euros the summer before, with England's Three Lions going all the way to the final, only to be defeated in a painful penalty shootout. Now the nation's hopes of a trophy rested on the shoulders of the Lionesses. Could Sarina's side forge their own way to Wembley? Not since 1984 had England's women reached a final, a time when none of the current squad of players was even born!

When Sarina announced a new captain for the tournament, Mary was thrilled; twenty-five-year-old Leah Williamson would stand in for the injured Steph Houghton. It didn't matter whether you played for Arsenal (Leah's club), Chelsea, one of the Manchester clubs or further afield, Leah made everyone feel loved and respected.

And as for Sarina, Mary had never worked with a coach quite like her. Since becoming England's head coach a few months ago, Sarina had brought the team together and set England on an unbeaten run of fourteen games. She had led her home nation the Netherlands to Euros success the last time around too, but could she do it again? Ask any of her Lionesses and 'yes' would be the answer!

Their adventure would begin at Old Trafford, Manchester United men's home ground. Mary had played there for the first time with her club the previous season – it was a dream come true to play on such an amazing pitch, but under COVID-19 rules, no fans had been allowed inside the ground. This time, the stadium would be rocking for the game against Austria. Mary couldn't wait!

What an occasion! England were nervy, but ran out 1–0 winners thanks to a goal from Beth Mead amid lashing rain and fireworks. Mary had played her part in the win too, making a vital reaction save to keep out Austrian Barbara Dunst's shot.

Norway next, a tougher opposition on paper, but

England powered past them scoring an incredible eight goals!

Georgia Stanway, Lauren Hemp, Alessia, two for Ellen and a hat-trick for Beth – not bad! Mary counted the goalscorers.

At the other end of the pitch, Mary barely had a save to make, but had promised herself that nothing would get past her that night.

Another goal-fest followed in England's final group match. A final score of 5–0 to the Lionesses against Northern Ireland saw them sail through to the knockouts having easily scored more goals than any other nation. What's more, Mary had kept three clean sheets out of three!

CHAPTER 15

MARY, QUEEN OF STOPS

Everything had gone according to plan for the Lionesses so far, but their next opponents Spain were more than capable of ending England's fairy tale. Even without their superstars Alexia Putellas and Jenni Hermoso, *La Roja* were still tipped as one of the tournament favourites.

Spain set out their stall from the start, with Mary called into action straight away. When she burst out of goal to claim a cross, the English crowd erupted in cheers.

'MARY! MARY! MARY!' they chanted.

Wow! thought Mary. They were cheering just for her, and it felt amazing!

After seventeen minutes, she followed with another save with her feet. England's Number 1 made it look easy! Chance after chance followed for Spain, but it was Ellen who was first to find the back of the net, until...

'Noooo! Offside!' Mary spotted the assistant referee's flag.

Half-time arrived with the scoreboard still showing 0–0. England would have to be patient in the second half and create some more goal-scoring opportunities.

After the break, the Lionesses looked much livelier, pushing forwards with some neat passing in search of a goal. But it was Spain who scored first, Bonmatí and Cardona stretching England's defence to allow González to stroke the ball past Mary in the fifty-fourth minute. They almost grabbed a second soon after, but this time Mary stuck out a strong hand to stop Del Castillo's dipping effort. The crowd suddenly fell silent. England had to fight back – or they would be out.

On came Mary's Manchester United teammates Alessia and Ella to shake up England's attack. And with just minutes of the ninety left to play, Alessia knocked the ball down to Ella who smashed home a sensational volley. *Gooooooaaaaaaalllllllll!!!!!!!!!*

The match headed into extra time, with England now on top. Then when Georgia Stanway collected a loose pass in midfield, the space to shoot opened up in front of her and she buried the ball past Sandra Paños in goal. What a winner! Spain were sunk!

'Come on!' Mary bellowed at the final whistle, before leaping into Millie's arms.

'You were amazing today, Mearps!' Millie thanked her keeper.

Then came a Lionesses lap of honour for the fans – it was time to get the party started!

*

Having come from behind to knock Spain out in the quarters, England had the fans and the press believing that the trophy was theirs to lose. It felt like this special squad had the whole nation behind them. Sarina knew she had to keep her players grounded, it would be easy to get carried away.

'There's plenty of work still to be done,' Sarina explained. 'We'll carry on taking things one match at a time.'

The boss was right; now was not the time to let standards slip. Especially as the Olympic silver medallists Sweden stood between the Lionesses and their fairy-tale Wembley final. England would have to show their steel in Sheffield next.

Sweden started on the front foot, smashing a header against the crossbar early on.

'Wake up!' Mary screamed at her defence.

It wasn't until thirty-four minutes into the game when the deadlock was broken, thankfully by England!

Lucy collected the ball on the right wing and crossed to Beth who unleashed an unstoppable finish.

How many's that for Beth now? Mary wondered. It had to be at least six tournament goals! The fans were right – Meado was on fire!

But 1–0 was not going to be the final score; Mary could feel in her bones that were more goals to come.

She just hoped they would not be against her! In determined mood, England's super stopper pulled off a stunning save to deny Stina Blackstenius from close range.

Leah pumped her fists. 'Yes, Mary!'

Then came a chance for Lucy at the other end, and her header bounced up off the ground and into the net. The fans were on their feet, as choruses of 'Sweet Caroline' rang out around the ground.

With a comfortable 2–0 cushion, England really turned on the style next. Fran Kirby squared a pass to Alessia, who saw her shot saved in a crowded box. She wasn't about to give up though and tried a cheeky backheel... that went straight through the keeper's legs! *Goooooooaaaaallllll!!!!!!* ALESSIA RUSSO!

'A backheel and a nutmeg in one shot!' Mary couldn't wait to give her teammate a huge hug.

And when Fran scored her own showstopper late on, the sea of yellow shirts in the far stand was silenced for good. 4–0!

They had done it; the Lionesses were into the Euros final! What a night! England's goalscorers had got them over the line, but Mary's saves had kept her team in the tournament on more than one occasion that match. She had definitely earned her latest nickname: 'Mary, Queen of Stops'!

Sarina was the first to congratulate her keeper after the match. 'Well done, Mary,' she said. 'You were incredible tonight!'

'I can't thank you enough for believing in me!' Mary replied happily. She would always be grateful to Sarina for giving her a second chance; Mary couldn't imagine not being a part of this team of brave Lionesses.

They were just one victory away from winning the nation's first major football trophy in fifty-six years. Was football coming home? Of course it was!

CHAPTER 16

CELEBRATIONS INCOMING!

Sandwiched between her defenders Millie and Leah for the national anthems, Mary was the only Lioness with her jacket unzipped. Her bright green jersey stood out against her teammates' gleaming white kits. She wanted everyone to know how proud she was of being a goalkeeper. It was such a special position.

Thankfully, Mary didn't feel nervous at all. She had woken up confident of an England win. The team had worked so hard to get to Wembley, with some amazing victories along the way. Now just one team stood between the Lionesses and the trophy.

Germany. European champions a record eight times, they had already knocked out Netherlands and

France to get to the final. England, meanwhile, had never won the tournament. Beating their rivals would be no mean feat, but with the match on home soil, the Lionesses and their fans believed that anything was possible.

Soon after the team photos, Germany were forced to make a late change to their starting eleven. Their star striker and Mary's old teammate at Wolfsburg, Alex Popp, had pulled up injured after the warm-up.

What a miss she'll be! thought Mary, but there were plenty of other players on the pitch who could cause England problems.

By half-time, the best of the game's chances had fallen to England, with Ellen and Lucy getting shots on target. Meanwhile, Mary was forced to make a crucial stop on the line to deny Germany's Marina Hegering.

After the break, Lina Magull came close too, her shot whistling past Mary's right post. England were getting nervy – Sarina had to switch things up. On came Ella and Alessia for Fran and Ellen. Mary's young Manchester United teammates had done everything asked of them over the tournament so far.

On fifty-seven minutes, there was more danger for England… this time midfielder Lea Schüller was clean through on goal with only the keeper to beat. Mary raced to the ball, arriving a second ahead of the German, and scooped it up in her arms. SAVE!

Frustrated at missing her chance, Schüller kept on running and planted a sneaky stud on Mary. INJURY!

Wow, that hurt, thought Mary, clutching the ball to her chest. She lay there for a few moments, her right leg throbbing.

'Did you see that?' captain Leah asked the referee angrily.

The ref had – and brandished a yellow card to Schüller as Mary got back to her feet. It would take more than a late challenge to stop Mary Alexandra Earps!

The fans in the stands breathed a sizeable sigh of relief.

Then a big chance fell to England, as Keira picked out Ella with a pass that split Germany's defence. Ella found herself one-on-one with keeper Merle Frohms just minutes after coming on. Could she finish in front of 87,000 fans at Wembley? Yes, she could! Her cool chip over Frohms's head was worthy of any cup final! Talk about a super sub!

'The goalscorer for England, Number 20, ELLA TOOOOOOONE!' the stadium announcer boomed.

Mary pointed her gloved fingers at the heavens. *We can totally do this!* she believed.

But the half an hour that remained on the stopwatch felt like a lifetime. The game could change countless times before the final whistle.

Just minutes later, Germany hit back. Lina Magull's shot rattled the England crossbar, before Mary gathered the rebound confidently. SAVE! She lapped up the crowd's applause.

But in the seventy-ninth minute, the visitors did earn their equaliser. A cross from Tabea Wassmuth found Magull again, who connected perfectly from six yards. Mary could only watch in horror as the ball flew over her head and into the top-right corner.

'We go again,' Leah called, clapping her hands. England had to stay calm.

The match was on a knife-edge – it could be

that whichever side scored next would become European champions, unless the match was destined to end in a dreaded penalty shootout? It couldn't possibly, could it?

Noooo! Because with just ten minutes of extra time remaining, Chloe Kelly scrambled home an England corner to rapturous applause.

Goooooooaaaaaaaaallllllll!!!!!!! The substitute ripped off her shirt and began swinging it around her head like a lasso. A yellow card for the celebration followed, but Chloe didn't complain.

Now England had the lead again, they were determined not to surrender it.

Mary watched through gritted teeth. *Hold on to the ball! Hold on to the ball!* she willed her team.

Then came a welcome sound, shrill yet so sweet: the final whistle had been blown!

ENGLAND WERE EUROPEAN CHAMPIONS AND FOOTBALL HAD COME HOME!

Mary dropped to the floor in sheer exhaustion, lying

for a moment with two pumped fists.

Incredible scenes followed. There were tears, hugs and Lionesses dancing as the crowd sang 'Sweet Caroline'.

England accepted their gold medals proudly before Leah and Millie lifted the sleek glass trophy. As confetti rained down and fireworks boomed, everything about that moment was perfect.

After celebrating with the fans in the stadium, the players carried on the party in the dressing room and beyond. No one minded that the Lionesses were all still in their sweaty kits and socks!

'Come on, girls,' said Lucy. 'We're going to crash Sarina's press conference!'

So the players followed Lucy's cue and congaed into the conference room, where the world's journalists had gathered.

'It's coming home, it's coming home, football's coming home!' the Lionesses chanted.

Mary suddenly found herself climbing onto Sarina's desk and began dancing wildly, while a sea of smartphones recorded the scene.

Sarina looked up at her like an embarrassed mum.

Oops, thought Mary. *What must the gaffer be thinking? Too late now!* She carried on her jig for a few more seconds, before making a sheepish exit.

The day of the final was quite simply the best day of Mary's life, and the days and weeks that followed were one big happy blur. To have worked towards something for so long and achieved the goal she'd set felt almost magical. Mary was voted the tournament's best keeper, while the whole squad of Lionesses became official football legends overnight!

'If I could bottle this feeling, I would take a little sip every day,' Mary told the press. She had never been happier.

CHAPTER 17

THE BEST

By the spring of 2023, the Lionesses had stretched their unbeaten run to an incredible twenty-nine games, and picked up more silverware too. The Arnold Clark Trophy belonged to England for the second year running, after they roared to victory against South Korea, Italy and Belgium.

The Belgium game had been the pick of the bunch, as England ran out 6–1 winners in Bristol. Sarina was happy, the fans were thrilled, but one Lioness was livid… Mary.

When Belgian sub Elena Dhont smashed her shot past Mary into the far corner in stoppage time, the England keeper was furious with herself. Mary's chance to claim a clean sheet had just gone up in smoke, and she stamped on the turf in disgust, shaking her head.

To be fair, it was a beautiful strike that ninety-nine out of a hundred keepers couldn't have saved, but Mary was disappointed she had conceded all the same.

In the post-match huddle, the Lionesses couldn't let Mary's tantrum go unpunished and set about some friendly teasing.

'How'd it go again, Mazza?' mocked Georgia Stanway. 'Like this, right?' She stamped one foot forcefully on the ground.

Mary was shoved into the middle of the huddle and pretended to hang her head in shame. 'I'm sorry! I'm sorry!' she cried, beginning to giggle at last.

'We just won 6–1,' Leah reassured her. 'Don't worry about one goal. Besides, it was one heck of a shot!'

Mary was used to the banter, and she always gave as good as she got, but she wouldn't have changed her competitive nature for a second – it was part of what made her so good.

Exactly how brilliant a goalkeeper Mary had become

was about to be established the very next week.

*

England duty done, Mary's next destination was Paris a few days later, alongside her Lioness teammates Lucy, Beth, Jess Carter and boss Sarina. They had been invited to FIFA's Best Football Awards ceremony, a glitzy affair to celebrate the achievements of the world's greatest male and female players. Of course that meant a new outfit; Mary opted for a shimmering sequinned dress, matched with heels the size of small skyscrapers.

As she took her seat in the Salle Pleyel, an elegant concert hall, Mary felt like a little kid again. Everywhere she looked there was a baller! From Lionel Messi and Kylian Mbappé to Alexia Putellas and Alex Morgan. Football royalty had gathered, and Mary was rubbing shoulders with them all!

In the very first award, Mary faced some stiff competition for the Best FIFA Women's Goalkeeper. The top keepers from Spain, Germany, United States and Chile had all been nominated and Mary fully expected Chile's Christiane Endler to win for a second time.

So when 'MARY EARPS' was announced as the winner, her jaw almost hit the floor. She tottered towards the stage, repeating, *'Don't trip over, don't trip over!'* under her breath.

Her old friend and the ceremony host for the evening, Jermaine Jenas, gallantly helped Mary onto the stage.

'I so shouldn't have worn this dress!' she whispered to him, nervously.

She hadn't thought to prepare any sort of acceptance speech, so had to think fast. Luckily, Mary had never been afraid of speaking up. All she could do was to talk from the heart. So, with the surprisingly heavy trophy in her arms, Mary kicked off her list of thank yous.

'To my loved ones, who picked me up off the kitchen floor a few years ago,' she began, before thanking her teammates, coaching staff and of course, Sarina. 'This is for anyone who has been in a dark place, just know that there's light at the end of the tunnel, *keep going...*' the words tumbled out. 'Sometimes success looks like this, collecting trophies sometimes it's just waking up and putting one step in front of the other. There's only one of you in the world and that's more than enough – be unapologetically yourself.'

What a speech! There wasn't a dry eye in the house! The TV cameras panned to Sarina, who was bursting with pride for her player, while the Lionesses led the whoops and cheers.

All the world's press wanted to interview Mary after the ceremony – she was a hero! Standing on the green carpet, she cradled the trophy in her arms like a baby, beaming. The whole evening felt like a dream. But it was official – Mary was the best women's goalkeeper in the world. 'Somebody pinch me!' she joked.

One thing was for sure: her luggage for the flight home had just got a whole lot heavier.

CHAPTER 18

FINALISSIMA 2023

It wasn't long before the Lionesses were back in action, this time in a fixture that would see the European champions battle it out with South American champions Brazil for the chance to add a brand-new trophy to their fast-growing collection.

More than 83,000 tickets had been sold for the Finalissima as England returned to Wembley Stadium for the first time, the scene of their incredible smash-and-grab victory over Spain. Being back at Wembley felt like home and the team were hungry to make some more special memories and do the nation proud. The task ahead of them would be far from easy, though – legends Ellen and Jill had both hung up their boots after the Euros final, retiring on a high, while Beth, Fran and vice-captain Millie were all out injured. Brazil meanwhile were a technically brilliant side, full of smart and experienced players.

So, could England claim another trophy and extend their unbeaten streak to thirty matches? There wasn't even a flicker of doubt in Mary's mind as she walked out onto the pitch. Win or lose, though, she felt so lucky to be part of this team.

'We can totally do this!' she boomed, as the national anthem came to an end. She clapped her huge, gloved hands together loudly. The home crowd believed it too.

England's players stripped off to reveal their gleaming white shirts, while Mary was in full salmon-pink for the evening. It was a first outing for the new kit, the same kit they would wear for the World Cup that summer.

The match unfolded as a game of two halves. The first forty-five saw England dominate, with Lauren Hemp and Alessia looking lively up front. But despite their pressure, only Ella was able to find the back of the net by the break. Lauren James had smashed home a spectacular shot, but the flag went up straight away. Unlucky!

The second half saw Brazil change tactics, pressing forwards in search of an equaliser. Barcelona forward Geyse came close with a long-range strike for the visitors, but Mary was alert to it, palming the shot onto the crossbar and safely away.

Then in stoppage time, the unthinkable happened. Mary made a mistake that proved she was human, after all. When the Brazil forward drilled her cross into the six-yard box, it looked like an easy stop to make, but somehow the ball squirmed out of the England goalkeeper's grasp and there was Brazil sub Andressa Alves to smash the ball into the roof of the net.

Gutted! 1–1 in the dying seconds of the game.

OK, how am I going to bounce back from this? Mary asked herself. She was desperate to make up for her blunder. As luck would have it, the stage was set for goalkeepers to become heroes – the match was skipping extra time to go straight to a penalty shootout. Here was her chance to redeem herself;

Mary was ready.

Georgia struck first to put England ahead, her shot just too strong for the Brazil keeper. But Adriana levelled the scores when her strike hit Mary's hand and went in. So close to a save!

Then when Ella's weak penalty was saved, the pressure was well and truly on. Mary had to step up! And step up she did, saving Tamires's low strike to her left.

'Listen to the crowd!' Chelsea manager Emma Hayes said on the commentary, as Wembley erupted into a roar of relief.

Rachel Daly dispatched the perfect penalty next for the Lionesses, while Rafaelle could only find the crossbar. Advantage England! Then when Alex Greenwood and Kerolin each scored for their sides, Chloe had the chance to wrap up another famous Lionesses victory. Could she do it? She certainly could! With a skip and a hop, the Manchester City winger rifled home her penalty. England had done it, they had won the Finalissma 2023 trophy, while Mary had gone from villain to hero in the space of minutes.

Mary was buzzing! Any little kids watching that performance, inside the stadium or on TV back home, couldn't fail to be inspired. She hoped she had shown just how special goalkeeping could be.

Then it was time for the trophy lift and fireworks. Winning trophies would never get old, and this one was extra special – as vice-captain for the evening, Mary got to raise the shiny silver cup to the crowd with Leah.

Wow! thought Mary. Moments like this felt beyond her wildest dreams. If you'd have told that little girl from Nottinghamshire that this night was in her future, she would probably have exploded with excitement.

Their fifth trophy under Sarina, the Lionesses marched on towards the summer in pursuit of a sixth. The Big One: the Women's World Cup.

CHAPTER 19

A SEASON TO REMEMBER

Back at Manchester United, Mary was having another
excellent season. The side was settled, and manager
Marc Skinner wouldn't have swapped his goalkeeper
for anyone else in the world. With Ona Batlle, Maya
Le Tissier and Millie Turner in front of Mary, the
Red Devils formed the meanest defence in the whole
league. The club's fine form saw them top the table for
a large part of the season, with Chelsea having played
one game fewer, while fans had flooded into Old
Trafford for the two games showcased there.

There was a cup run to delight the fans too, as wins
against Sunderland, Durham, Lewes and Brighton &
Hove Albion set up a day out at Wembley for United's

first ever FA Women's Cup final in May 2023. The sell-out crowd of 77,390 set a new record for a women's domestic cup match, while the atmosphere inside the stadium was electric.

Mary was buzzing too. By now, the goalkeeper knew how to handle the big occasions and only felt excitement when she stepped out onto the enormous Wembley pitch. For some of her teammates, though, a first trip to Wembley came with nerves that would have to be quickly quelled.

'You've got this,' she told young defender Maya Le Tissier. 'Once you've had a few touches, you'll be fine. You'll love it, I promise!'

The team was well organised, determined and hungry for success, so why shouldn't they feel confident? Only one team stood between them and a first FA Cup trophy. Unfortunately, that team was Chelsea, a side that United had *never* beaten, and the only side to have defeated the Red Devils in the league that season. Twice. But this was a cup final, a one-off game that either side could win. Chelsea may have been the favourites, but every underdog has its day.

United almost got off to a dream start when Leah Galton pounced on a fumbled clearance from a Chelsea defender and slotted home. The Red half of Wembley let out a roar of half surprise, half joy, until they spotted a late flag from the referee's assistant. Offside!

Shame, thought Mary. *We almost caught them napping there!*

Both teams went on to create chances: Millie Turner came close for United, while Mary was called into action to tip a looping header from Chelsea's Lauren James onto the post.

With an hour played, Chelsea looked tired. Fresh legs were needed. When it came to the bench, Chelsea's subs were far stronger. Pernille Harder entered the play, making an immediate impact when her ball to the far post found Sam Kerr in space, who broke the deadlock at last.

Nooooooooooo!

Every time Kerr played against Mary, she scored, like a terrible ghost sent to haunt the keeper. Mary threw her arms up in frustration. It had been an easy finish in the end. The defence had completely switched off – something you couldn't do for a second when a striker of Sam Kerr's quality was in the box. Out came the Australian's famous backflip celebration. Mary couldn't watch.

A final chance to equalise came after the ninety minutes were up, but Alessia could only scuff her shot into the Chelsea goalkeeper's arms. Then it was over. Wembley was blue. A painful lesson for Mary and her team, but it was only one that would make them stronger.

'We'll be back here one day,' Mary promised the fans, sounding as positive as ever. 'We gave it our all, but Chelsea's experience paid off on the day,'

*

Back in the league, a single point separated Manchester United and Chelsea as the teams headed into the business end of the season. Although United topped the table, Chelsea could leapfrog them if they won their game in hand.

Even if they did finish as runners-up, it had been an

unforgettable season for Marc Skinner's side. Doing the double over rivals Arsenal showed just how far United had come since Mary had joined the club, while a first win over neighbours Man City in May was a derby that delivered! A record crowd gathered at Leigh Sports Village in the hope of seeing United keep their title hopes alive and they did not go home disappointed. Hayley Ladd's rocket-powered shot gave the home side an early lead, until Filippa Angeldahl's surprise equaliser threatened to spoil the party. The cross to the far post had caught Mary off-guard and gone straight in, leaving the keeper floored. Nightmare!

'Keep going!' Mary tried to rouse her teammates. 'We go again.'

If United couldn't score again, the Women's Super League trophy would be staying in London, with Chelsea crowned champions for the fourth time in a row. It was beginning to look inevitable, until United sub Lucía García came on. Would she be the one to save Mary's blushes? Yes, she would! When a cutback fell into her path, the Spanish forward somehow managed to bundle the ball home.

Goooooooooaaaaaaaaallllllll!!!!!!

If Chelsea were going to win the league, it wasn't going to be today! Manchester United had pulled it out of the bag in stoppage time. The title would be decided on the last day of the season.

In the end, both clubs won, United beating Liverpool away with another Lucía García winner and a clean sheet for Mary, while Chelsea never looked like slipping up against already-relegated Reading. Chelsea were champions, but United proudly finished second – their highest-ever league position – earning them a spot in the Champions League.

Mary had completed another fantastic season too. She had been a brick wall in goal all season long! If her defenders ever made a mistake, Mary was usually there to mop up the mess. She just hated conceding goals! Her fourteen league clean sheets set a new WSL record, earning her the Golden Glove.

Now all she had to do was to carry the form of her life over to her country, as the Women's World Cup drew closer.

CHAPTER 20

DREAMING DOWN UNDER

When England finally touched down in Australia, it felt very different for Mary from the last time she had arrived at a World Cup. Four years earlier, she had been on the fringes of the Lionesses squad for France 2019 and hadn't kicked (or caught) a single ball. Fast forward to 2023, and she was now England's vice-captain for the tournament and had grown into one of the best players in the whole world. Her journey had been nothing short of epic.

Mary and the team had set themselves a big goal. 'We're here to win this tournament,' the Lionesses said in their interviews. It would be tough to beat teams like United States, Sweden and Spain, but

England believed that with their talent and teamwork they could really challenge for the trophy.

While the team waited for their jet lag from the long flight from London to settle down, the Lionesses spent their days on Australia's Sunshine Coast whale watching, cuddling koalas and posting plenty of dance routines on social media. Some of the memories they were making together would last a lifetime.

With training perfectly on track too, there was just one thing that was frustrating Mary, and that was happening off the pitch. While the Lionesses home and away shirts were on sale in all different sizes, England goalkeeper shirts were rarer than a Mary Earps goal! Fans could pick up a 'BRONZE 2', 'WALSH 6' or 'HEMP 11' shirt to wear while cheering on the girls, but Mary's shirt with 'EARPS 1' on the back was not on sale in any shops.

Mary felt very hurt. She hadn't been able to order any shirts for her friends and family, like the rest of the squad, but worse, what about all those kids out there who were dreaming of becoming goalkeepers? She had to use her voice and speak out before the World

Cup kicked off. So Mary took on the kit manufacturer in a press conference, while a petition went viral, with hundreds of thousands of people adding their support. In the end, the company backed down and agreed to make and sell England goalkeeper shirts – but they wouldn't be ready until after the tournament. Victory!

*

A couple of days later, it was time for the football to begin at last. Mary was itching to play.

In England's opening Group D match against Haiti, the Lionesses made a stuttering start. Haiti were a physical side with some talented teenagers in their line-up. Playing in their first World Cup, the Caribbean team were keen to make their mark.

In the first half, England were handed a huge slice of luck when a Haiti forward tried to stop a cross in the box... using both hands. Penalty!

Georgia, usually so reliable from the spot, took aim. But Haiti's keeper Kerly Théus dived to her right and palmed the ball away to safety. SAVE! Her teammates rushed to congratulate her... but wait – Théus had left her line too soon! Georgia calmly dispatched the retake, this time burying her shot. GOAL!

The second half saw the goalkeepers tested at either end, Théus saving a string of attempts on goal from Alessia, while Mary stood firm to keep out some goal-bound efforts from Haiti before the final whistle. It hadn't been a vintage Lionesses performance, but three points on the board and a clean sheet were exactly what they needed to kickstart their tournament.

A second clean sheet followed against Denmark, as England ground out another narrow win. A wonder strike from Lauren James, a solid save from Mary and a helpful goalpost saw the match end 1–0. Three more points, but England would have to move up the gears if they wanted to go far in the competition.

Their last group match saw England finally find their form, firing six past China in a performance worthy of their European champions status. Alessia, Lauren Hemp, Chloe and Rachel all got on the scoresheet, while Lauren James dazzled with a double.

Mary was annoyed she'd been beaten from the spot, awarded after an unfortunate handball on the line from Lucy, the only blip in a brilliant Lionesses performance.

But with three wins from three, eight goals scored and only one conceded, the Lionesses could be satisfied with their start to the tournament as they marched on into the knockout rounds.

CHAPTER 21

INTO THE KNOCKOUTS

The knockout rounds, where only a win would do. Of the thirty-two teams that had entered the tournament, only half now remained. Titans Germany and Brazil had sensationally failed to get through, and nor had Olympic champions Canada, although World Cup holders United States had ridden their luck to reach the final sixteen teams. It was a huge wake-up call to the teams that were left – even a small slip-up and they could be on the plane home too.

Nigeria, ranked thirty-six places below England in the world, were aiming to create some shockwaves of their own. Victory over the European Champions would be one of the biggest upsets in World

Cup history.

'Let's stay focused from the first whistle,' Mary told her defenders, as a swirl of nervous energy bubbled up inside her stomach.

And she was right to worry; her first touch was a nervy punch, while the crossbar saved England's blushes next after a smart strike from Nigeria's Plumptre. Play continued with Nigeria looking the more dangerous side, forcing England deeper and deeper into their own half. Was this the same England team that had scored six on their last outing? The goals had dried up completely.

The game was still goalless with three minutes to go, when a frustrated Lauren James got in a tangle with her marker. While Alozie lay on the ground, Lauren deliberately stepped on the Nigerian defender.

The ref's yellow card was quickly upgraded to red by VAR, as Lauren trudged off the pitch, leaving England down to ten players. Nightmare!

What a silly thing to do! thought Mary. *Lashing out could cost us our whole World Cup. You just can't do things like that.*

Lauren knew what she had done was wrong straightaway and accepted her punishment. That split-second mistake would haunt her for a long time.

Meanwhile, England's ten Lionesses clung on for thirty minutes of extra time for penalties. Five penalty kicks each to decide which team would go through to the quarter-finals. England won the toss and chose to go first.

Georgia stepped up, but saw her strike fly wide of the left-hand post. MISS!

But Nigeria could only reply with a carbon copy of Georgia's penalty. Another MISS! Georgia was off the hook.

Thankfully, Bethany England buried her spot-kick next, before a weary-looking Alozie placed the ball on the spot for Nigeria.

She's not scoring this, Mary thought to herself, feeling ten feet tall. And sure enough, Alozie smashed it over the bar!

Rachel Daly was never going to miss next. Her mighty pen gave Nnadozie no chance. Unstoppable!

With the pressure on Nigeria, Ajibade pulled a

goal back when Mary dived over the ball. The Super Falcons were not going out without a fight.

But when Alex Greenwood – who had been superb all game – sent Nnadozie the wrong way next, Mary had the chance to make the winning save.

It wasn't to be just yet – Mary stood rooted to the spot as Nigeria's Ucheibe netted neatly. She hadn't seen that one coming.

So it was over to Chloe Kelly to try to win it for England, and win it she did! With her trademark, hop, skip and jump, Chloe blasted her penalty through the goalkeeper's gloves and into the back of the net. What a rocket!

England were through... by the skin of their teeth.

'I'm so tired, but really chuffed that we got the job done!' Mary told the press after the match. 'Our best performance is yet to come,' she promised.

CHAPTER 22

MATILDAS MATCH-UP

So far in Australia, luck had been on the side of the Lionesses, appearing just when they needed it most. The thing about luck though, Mary knew well, is that sooner or later it always ran out. The Nigeria game had been their worst performance of their World Cup so far, with Lauren's sending off a low point, but they were still in the tournament and that was what counted.

Sarina was right – they would have to hold on to the ball better, create more chances and make fewer sloppy mistakes next time, or England would surely be out.

Five days later, the Lionesses were looking forward to starting afresh against Colombia. Sarina didn't need to say too much in the dressing room; every player knew what was at stake.

'How do you say it... a clean slate?' Sarina told her team. 'It will be tough, but I expect us to win.'

The Lionesses' Dutch coach wasn't wrong about the tough task that lay ahead. So far, Colombia had eliminated Germany from their group and seen off Jamaica in their Round of 16 tie. Mary and her teammates were not about to underestimate a team with talented teen Linda Caicedo and Atlético's Leicy Santos in their ranks.

England looked sharp from the kick-off, but it was Colombia who shocked the European Champions by taking a first-half lead: Santos showed off some tricky footwork on the edge of the box before curling a lob that sailed into the tiny space between Mary's glove and the crossbar. GOAL! The mass of yellow shirts in the Sydney crowd celebrated wildly.

It had taken a very special goal to do it, but Mary had at last been beaten in open play for the first time in the whole tournament. She felt terrible, but was determined that would be the only goal she would concede that night. England weren't used to finding themselves behind, though. Did the Lionesses have what it took to turn things around?

Yes! Lauren Hemp lifted the mood in the dying seconds of the first half. When Colombia's keeper Pérez spilled the ball, it was Lauren who stabbed home the equaliser in a goalmouth scramble. A scrappy but very welcome goal. *1–1!*

And when Alessia delivered a deadly turn and finish on sixty-three minutes, England resolved to hold on to their lead at all costs.

Colombia fought back bravely, Bedoya trying her luck from distance. The ball swerved in the air, but Mary was equal to it, and tipped over spectacularly. A nervy end to the match followed, as England battled to keep out Colombia's classy attackers.

Then in her box, Mary let out a huge roar of relief. Full time! Colombia had pushed them all the way, but it was England who had sealed their semi-final spot with a much better performance this round.

The tournament joint-hosts Australia would be England's opponents in the semis. With the whole nation behind them, the Matildas would take some beating. A friendly defeat to the Aussies that spring was still fresh in the minds of the Lionesses, the only team to have beaten them since Sarina had taken charge. England had more big-match experience, but Australia had the support of a home crowd. The stage was set for a serious contest.

The big news from the Australia camp was that their superstar striker and captain, Sam Kerr, who had barely played since tearing her calf muscle on the eve of the tournament, was back in the starting line-up.

'Keep Sam Kerr quiet and we can do this,' Mary instructed her defence. But there were plenty more Aussie attackers keen to get on the scoresheet.

England held on to the ball well early on, before Ella opened the scoring after thirty-six minutes to give England a worthy lead. Her drilled shot into the top corner silenced Stadium Australia, but for a section of white whose cheers were even louder than Mary's: *'TOOOOOOONE!'*

So far, so good. England were on top, but Sam Kerr was on the pitch – she could conjure up a goal from nothing at any moment. And that's precisely what she did. Just past the hour mark, Mary's nemesis received the ball in her own half before turning swiftly. With her Chelsea teammates Millie and Jess on the back foot, on ran Kerr unchallenged until she let fly from twenty-five yards out. The ball skimmed Millie's knee on its way past Mary into the net.

Gooooooooooooaaaaaaaaaaaaaaalllllllll!!!!!!!!!
Stadium Australia erupted like never before.

'Why didn't you close her down? You know how good she is!' is what Mary wanted to scream at her teammates, but she knew it wouldn't achieve anything. It was a goal worthy of a Hollywood movie, somehow written in the stars. She was used to Kerr terrorising her in the WSL, but now the Aussie had done it again on the world stage too. *Not fair!*

England quickly regrouped, desperate to retake the lead. And eight minutes later, their efforts were rewarded. Millie hit a hopeful ball into penalty area, only for it to bobble perfectly on to the left foot of Lauren Hemp. Hempo made no mistake in finding the corner of the net to edge England back in front.

Kerr wasted a golden opportunity next for Australia,

143

before Lauren Hemp decided it was time for another England goal. After a driving run, she took out four defenders with a perfect, angled pass to Alessia on the edge of the box. Alessia kept her cool and shot low across goal into the far corner. *3–1!* Incredible!

In the end, England waltzed past the Matildas comfortably.

They hadn't always been at their best this tournament, but the Lionesses had managed to beat teams from North America, Europe, Asia, Africa, South America and now Oceania to earn a place in their first ever World Cup final. What a journey!

Then came the final, where the Lionesses' luck ran out at last. Lauren Hemp hit the bar early on, but after that England chances were few and far between. Once Olga Carmona's well-taken goal had put Spain ahead, Mary's epic performance and massive penalty save gave England hope right up until the moment that the final whistle blew. In the end, though, it just wasn't England's day. Spain were crowned the new world champions, while England had to make do with silver medals.

CHAPTER 23

SOMETHING ABOUT MARY

As the dust settled from the World Cup, feelings of disappointment began to turn into feelings of pride among the Lionesses. The result wasn't what Mary and the team had set out to achieve, but to play in a World Cup final had been the stuff of dreams.

'Spain are a fantastic team. We were beaten by the better side in that game if we're honest – there's no shame in that,' Mary said, reflecting on England's defeat.

And once she'd had chance to rest, Mary returned to training with Manchester United with even more fire in her belly.

Towards the end of the summer, it was reported

that Arsenal had tried to bring Mary to London. There were rumours that the Gunners had made a world-record bid for the keeper. As far as Manchester United were concerned, though, Mary was one of their best players. She was definitely not for sale.

'That's the end of that then,' Mary thought to herself. All she wanted to do was to concentrate on playing well for her club, but the rumours wouldn't go away.

'Mary wants to leave United!' some reports said, which simply wasn't true.

Her patience was quickly running thin.

'We can't control what the media says,' her coach Marc Skinner told her. 'So let's put all that drama to one side and have a great season.'

His words were music to Mary's ears! In a couple of weeks' time, the club would make its debut in the Women's Champions League and Mary couldn't wait.

United had the home advantage in the first leg of their double-header against Paris Saint-Germain. Mary had to pull out a huge save in the first half, but she couldn't keep out Tabitha Chawinga in the second half. Thankfully, United's new signing Melvine Malard struck back to make it all square for the away leg in Paris.

United had to come from behind again at the Parc des Princes, but PSG were hungry for the win and retook the lead from the kick-off. Things went from bad to worse when Sandy Baltimore chipped Mary from a tight angle next and a perfectly good Manchester United equaliser was ruled out for a foul on the keeper. With the score 4–2 on aggregate, there was no coming back for Manchester United. Sadly, the Red Devils' Champions League adventure was over in a flash.

*

England's first game after the 2023 World Cup, meanwhile, had come just a month later, in the Nations League, a new competition that mirrored the men's version. The competition would decide which European nations qualified for the Olympics in Paris the following summer.

England's hopes of entering as Team GB began to slip away when they lost to the Netherlands and had a horror story on Halloween against Belgium.

By the time England met the Netherlands again in December 2023, nothing less than a victory would do. Worse still, the Lionesses would have to play without their captain Millie, out with an injured knee, while Leah Williamson was still months away from making her own return. Instead, Sarina had just the person in mind to lead her team: Mary!

Mary Earps, England captain, Mary thought to herself when Sarina broke the news. *This is literally a dream come true!* What's more, she would wear the armband at a packed Wembley Stadium!

Mary's first game as skipper did not disappoint, as England battled back from two goals down, before Ella did what she does best and completed an incredible second-half England comeback! 3–2 at Wembley under the lights. It didn't get much better than that! Mary punched the air in delight.

Her chances of going to the Olympics with Team GB were now slim, but not completely impossible.

If the Netherlands lost their next game and England scored loads against Scotland, there was a small chance that they could still head to Paris.

Four days later, the Lionesses pulled out another incredible performance, this time against home nations rivals Scotland. Sadly though, even six goals in Glasgow were not enough – a Netherlands goal in the ninety-fifth minute in their game earned the Orange Lionesses the top spot in the group. England gathered in a heartbroken huddle to lick their wounds.

The defeat was a low point for Mary that month, but her year was to end on a spectacular high. Just before Christmas, in a fancy ceremony at the BBC, the public voted England's Number 1 their sporting Number 1 too – as the Sports Personality of the Year! It was the biggest and heaviest trophy that Mary had ever seen.

Then a few days later, it was announced that King Charles had included Mary in his New Year's Honours list. She could expect a trip to Buckingham Palace or Windsor Castle and another shiny medal in 2024!

What an amazing year! There had always been

something special about Mary and now the whole world knew it. If her football career ended tomorrow, she could retire happier than she ever thought possible. But the Queen of Stops was far from ready to hand over her golden gloves just yet – her fans would never forgive her! She wanted more clean sheets, more fingertip saves, more dives in the mud and of course more trophies.

'I haven't won the Champions League yet and there's another Women's Euro in 2025!' said Mary eagerly, as she talked through her next goals with her family.

'That's our girl!' her dad said with a smile. 'That's our Mary.'

Winners didn't stop, and Mary was a winner.

Read on for a sneak preview of
another brilliant football story
by Emily Stead. . .

WILLIAMSON

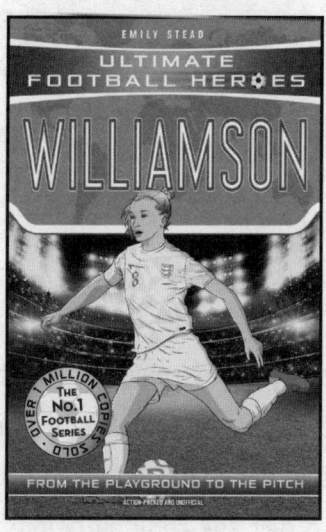

Available now!

CHAPTER 1

FINAL SCORE

31 July 2022, London
Women's Euro 2022 Final – England vs Germany

As Leah led her team of Lionesses onto the pitch, her usual game-face had been relegated to the dressing room. She was so happy to be at Wembley Stadium on this momentous day, she couldn't help but smile. The team had worked so hard to get to this final, winning every match on their way. Now England were ready to write a new chapter in women's football history, but first they'd have to defeat old enemies Germany.

A record crowd of 87,192 had packed into Wembley, with most of those supporting the

Lionesses. When the stadium announcer read out the teams, the fans cheered wildly. Every stand in the stadium was bouncing.

'Let's do our jobs girls, but let's enjoy every minute,' Leah told her teammates in the huddle. 'An occasion like this may never come around again.'

A few seconds more and the game would kick off. Leah looked down at her captain's armband, the same rainbow armband she had worn all tournament. She was skippering England at a Euros final on home soil. *This has to be a dream, doesn't it?* she wondered. *I'm going to wake up any minute now.*

The action got underway, with both teams creating early chances. England's best opportunities had fallen to Ellen White and Lucy Bronze, but they hadn't managed to get the ball over the line.

Then after twenty-seven minutes, it was England's goal that was suddenly under attack. In a goalmouth scramble, the ball bounced up and hit Leah on the shoulder. She didn't have her arms down like the rules said she was supposed to, so the game stopped for VAR to take a look. Was it a handball? It had happened in an instant; there was nothing Leah could have done, but penalties had been given for less. Time seemed to slow to a crawl while the check was completed. If VAR gave the penalty, Leah could go from hero to villain in the blink of an eye.

When the ref blew her whistle to play on at last, Leah breathed an enormous sigh of relief. Years ago, she wouldn't have been able to move past something like this, but now the England captain knew that dwelling on a mistake would get her nowhere. Instead, she stayed positive and carried on trying to help her team.

At half-time, 0–0 was a fair scoreline. Both sides had had moments of looking dangerous, but no one had managed to break through their defences. Whoever scored first would have to produce something special.

Soon after the break, Germany's Lina Magull fired a warning shot, but the ball pinged just wide of the post. Leah was calm but she could feel a nervous energy beginning to build around the stadium. England manager Sarina Wiegman responded by making a decisive double substitution, taking off experienced goalscorers Fran Kirby and Ellen While. Leah clapped their replacements Ella Toone and Alessia Russo onto the pitch, both of them fearless young Lionesses ready to give England their all.

Not long after, injury struck. England's top scorer of the tournament, Beth Mead, went down in a fifty-fifty tackle and couldn't carry on. Chloe Kelly replaced her.

'Stay positive,' Leah cried. 'Anyone on this pitch is capable of grabbing a goal.'

Then came a chance for England, as Keira Walsh picked out Ella with an outrageous defence-splitting pass. Ella was through on goal with just the keeper to beat. And without a flicker, the super sub scooped the ball high over German keeper Merle Frohms.

Goooooooooaaaaaaaaaaaalllllllllll!

'The goalscorer for England, Number 20, ELLA TOOOOOOONE!'

The cheers were so loud, they nearly lifted the Wembley roof off, arch and all!

Now 1–0 up, England had to settle quickly. With half an hour still to play, they were far from home and dry. Minutes later Germany rattled the England crossbar, before keeper Mary Earps gratefully swallowed up the rebound. Germany couldn't come much closer than that without scoring.

At last, in the seventy-ninth minute, the visitors' efforts were rewarded when forward Lina Magull equalised.

'We go again,' Leah rallied the England team. This match was far from over. In fact, if the scores stayed the same, thirty more minutes of extra time would be played.

Please not penalties, the thought flashed through Leah's mind.

But penalties weren't needed, because with just ten minutes to go, Chloe stuck a boot out to prod the ball past Frohms. Was it offside? Definitely not! 2–1 to England! The substitute took off her shirt in sheer delight and began swinging it around her head like a lasso. A yellow card was shown for the celebration, but nothing could bring Chloe down from cloud nine!

Now just minutes remained to defend a lead more precious than the Crown Jewels; England were not about to give up that lead again. Lucy and Ella held onto the ball, dragging it out to the corner flags, while Chloe's dancing feet drew fouls. With each minute that passed, Germany became more frustrated. England, though, were untouchable.

Finally, the referee's whistle blew.

ENGLAND WERE EUROPEAN CHAMPIONS!!!

And on that whistle, Leah's legs seemed to fail her. She dropped to the ground, as goosebumps spiked all over her body. It wasn't a bad sensation, far from it. She wished she could have bottled that feeling.

Millie Bright came over to help her up.

'What have we done here?' Leah hugged her, captain to vice-captain.

'Just incredible!' Millie struggled to reply.

But before Leah could start the celebrations properly, she headed to the centre circle. Sitting on the pitch was Lena Oberdorf, one hand covering her tear-stained face. The gifted young German had run Leah ragged all match, and it was only right to show her respect. The two shared a hug and a smile before England's captain joined her team.

Then without warning, Leah's own happy tears began to flow and flow. Out came every emotion she had been storing up for weeks now: joy, pride, sheer relief, but most of all love.

Six-year-old Leah, who fell in love with football at first sight, could never in her wildest dreams have imagined a day like today. This was the stuff of fairy tales.

CHAPTER 2

GUNNERS VERSUS SPURS

March 1997, Newport Pagnell, Buckinghamshire

In the cosy lounge of the Williamson family home in Newport Pagnell, Amanda and Grandma Berny sat on one sofa, with David on the other.

A couple of days earlier, proud parents Amanda and David had welcomed their first child into the world: Leah Cathrine Williamson.

Baby Leah was now sleeping soundly on her mum's chest, while the family opened presents from well-wishers.

'She's a little beauty,' said Amanda's mum, Leah's Grandma Berny, stroking the back of the baby's head.

'Isn't she just,' Amanda agreed.

While Amanda had her hands full, Berny unwrapped a small parcel wrapped in tissue paper. Inside, was a tiny red cardigan with white cuffs. Berny held it up to show Amanda and David. 'This one will really suit her,' said Berny. 'Don't you think, David?'

'Definitely not!' said Dad, opening a second package. 'This lilywhite sleepsuit is more her style.'

They were of course talking about football. Berny and Amanda were loyal Arsenal fans, while David's side of the family all supported Tottenham Hotspur. It made for some very loud times around the TV whenever the two teams faced each other in the Premier League.

'She might not even like football,' suggested Amanda, though this baby had been quite the kicker inside her tummy these past few weeks.

'I doubt that in this family,' Berny replied, with a smile.

So, would it be Highbury or White Hart Lane? Time would tell.

Leah's first love though turned out to be

gymnastics. As a tiny tot on the bars and balance beam she showed she had plenty of strength, while her floor routines were graceful. She had taken up the sport aged two, to try to correct a problem with the way she walked. By the age of five, Leah was attending classes four times a week.

Sometimes at the end of the session, the coach would roll a football across the springy floor and let the girls have a kickaround. Leah always looked forward to the mini matches – she could easily dribble around the other players and loved to shoot too. Before long, she began nagging her parents to let her play football properly.

Not every club was keen to let a girl join, but Leah's mum, Amanda, kept searching until at last she found Leah a club in nearby Bletchley and took her along for a trial. The railway line ran right alongside the pitch at Scot Youth FC, so when the trains rattled past in the middle of a match, you couldn't even hear the ref's whistle.

'It's only boys at the moment,' the coach told Amanda before Leah's first session. 'But if she's good enough, she'll play.'

Amanda was glad she had found a coach who was willing to let Leah play, but some of the boys stared at her daughter like she had three heads!

Maybe this wasn't such a good idea? Amanda worried.

She didn't tell Leah at the time, but her own experiences of playing football as a young girl were still painful to think about. She had wanted to play so badly that she'd had to cut her hair and pretend to be a boy to escape the nasty comments from opposition teams and their parents. There was no way Leah was cutting off her beautiful blonde locks!

She looked down at her daughter, little Leah, who didn't look nervous, not one bit. She already had her game-face on and ran onto the pitch with the boys without looking back.

Ten minutes later, Leah had already scored twice.

'She's good,' said a small boy with blond spiky hair. 'She can be on our team!'

After that, the boys began to pass her the ball. And before long, it was like she had always been one of the team. The boys grew to love having Leah around, especially the blond one, Mason, who became her best friend.

Still, there were those parents who thought it wasn't right that a girl could be better than their sons – but Leah played on with a smile on her face. Amanda was just glad her daughter's introduction to football was a happier one than her own.

*

It soon became clear that Leah had skills that were far beyond those of the average six-year-old boy or girl. She could do things with a football that other children couldn't master until years later.

'She's a natural,' the coach at Scot Youth told Amanda. It was music to Mum's ears! 'Have you thought about a girls' team for her?'

He told her about a girls-only academy at Rushden and Diamonds. Their fancy-sounding Centre of Excellence gave the best girls in the area the chance to play together. Leah could blossom there. It had much better pitches and proper coaches rather than parent volunteers, and so would make the forty-four-mile round trip worthwhile.

So, when she was accepted at the new academy, Leah was delighted! She would miss the boys at Scot Youth, but this was a positive step on her journey to becoming a better footballer. She knew she was lucky that her mum and dad had the time to take her to the sessions and that they had a car to get her there – many young players didn't have those luxuries.

For the next couple of seasons, the family travelled back and forth to Diamonds after school, with matches at the weekend. When Grandma Berny was busy, Leah's brother Jacob, five years younger than Leah, had to tag along and chased his own little ball up and down the sidelines. Football was in the blood, it seemed.

'My coaches say I'm doing pretty well,' Leah reported back to her parents after training one day. 'I've just got to keep working hard.'

Hard work had never been a problem for Leah. She trained harder than any of the young footballers at the academy and listened carefully to every last instruction the coaches gave her. Combined with her natural talent, her efforts were beginning to pay off. In the two seasons since she'd joined Rushden and Diamonds, she had come on in leaps and bounds.

VfL Wolfsburg

🏆 German Women's Bundesliga: 2018–19

🏆 German Women's Cup: 2018–19

Manchester United

🏆 Women's FA Cup runner-up: 2022–23

England

🏆 SheBelieves Cup: 2019

🏆 UEFA Women's Championship: 2022

🏆 Arnold Clark Cup: 2022, 2023

🏆 Finalissima: 2023

🏆 FIFA Women's World Cup runner-up: 2023

Individual

🏆 PFA WSL Team of the Year: 2016–17, 2022–23

🏆 UEFA Women's Championship Team of the Tournament: 2022

🏆 The Best FIFA Women's Goalkeeper: 2022

🏆 Freedom of the City of London: 2022

🏆 Women's Super League Golden Glove: 2022–23

🏆 England Women's Player of the Year: 2022–23

🏆 FIFA Women's World Cup Golden Glove: 2023

🏆 Sunday Times Sportswoman of the Year: 2023

🏆 BBC Women's Footballer of the Year: 2023

🏆 BBC Sports Personality of the Year: 2023

🏆 IFFHS Women's World's Best Goalkeeper: 2023

🏆 IFFHS Women's World Team of the Year: 2023

🏆 Member of the Order of the British Empire: 2023

EARPS

27

THE FACTS

NAME: Mary Alexandra Earps

DATE OF BIRTH: 7 March 1993

PLACE OF BIRTH: Nottingham

NATIONALITY: English

BEST FRIENDS: Katie Zelem, Nikita Parris

CURRENT CLUB: Manchester United

POSITION: Goalkeeper

THE STATS

Height (cm):	173
Club appearances:	247
Club goals:	66
Club trophies:	2
International appearances:	45
International clean sheets:	24
International trophies:	5

  ★ ★ ★ **HERO RATING: 95** ★ ★ ★

GREATEST MOMENTS

1   31 JULY 2022,
ENGLAND 2–1 GERMANY

This day saw the Lionesses become history-makers
as they overcame old foes Germany to win their first
major trophy. The Women's Euro final played on home
soil at Wembley Stadium saw Mary at the top of her
game, as she delivered the bravest of goalkeeping
performances. An inspiration to thousands of young
keepers up and down the country!

20 AUGUST 2023, SPAIN 1–0 ENGLAND

Although luck was not on England's side in the World Cup final, the Lionesses did create some memorable moments, not least Mary's strong second-half penalty save from Jenni Hermoso that kept England in the game. A solo goal from Olga Carmona sealed the win for Spain, while Mary took home the tournament's Golden Glove trophy and a silver medal as consolation prizes.

6 APRIL 2023, ENGLAND 1–1 BRAZIL (4–2 PENS)

A game that perfectly illustrated Mary's winning mentality. After conceding a last-minute goal from Andressa Alves, the England goalkeeper summoned all her mental strength to stand tall in a penalty shootout and help seal glory for her team. The Lionesses won a brand-new trophy in dramatic style, their fourth under Sarina Wiegman.

22 JANUARY 2023, READING 0–1 MANCHESTER UNITED

This one was special as Mary put in an inspired performance in goal to mark a record fiftieth clean sheet in the Women's Super League. United's keeper was equal to anything Reading could throw at her, while teammate Rachel Williams's late goal nicked the win. United leapt to the top of the league, blowing the title race wide open. Epic!

7 AUGUST 2023, ENGLAND 0–0 NIGERIA (4–2 PENS)

Another Player of the Match performance for the England keeper came at the Women's World Cup in Australia as the Lionesses came close to a shock exit against the Super Eagles. Mary somehow managed to keep Nigeria's excellent attackers at bay for 120 minutes, as England played extra time with ten players. *Thou shalt not pass* was her motto in the penalty shootout as the Lionesses sneaked into the quarter-finals.

TEST YOUR KNOWLEDGE

QUESTIONS

1. With which youth academy team did Mary start out in football?

2. Which Lionesses played with Mary at Doncaster Rovers Belles?

3. Who were England's opponents the first time Mary started for the national team?

4. For which club did Mary feature in the German Women's Bundesliga?

5. Which coach and former Lioness brought Mary back to the Women's Super League in 2019?

6. How many FA Women's Cup finals has Mary played in?

7. Who did England defeat 4–2 on penalties in the 2023 Finalissima?

8. How many Women's World Cup squads has Mary appeared in?

9. Mary saved a penalty from which Spanish player in the Women's World Cup final in 2023?

10. Which gleaming trophy did Mary win at the 2023 Women's World Cup final in Australia and New Zealand?

11. What word is missing from Mary's nickname here: Mary, Queen of _____?

Answers below . . . No cheating!

1. *Leicester City.* **2.** *Millie Bright and Bethany England.* **3.** *Kazakhstan.* **4.** *VfL Wolfsburg.* **5.** *Casey Stoney.* **6.** *One.* **7.** *Brazil.* **8.** *Two.* **9.** *Jenni Hermoso.* **10.** *The Golden Glove.* **11.** *Stops.*

PLAY LIKE YOUR HEROES

HOW TO COMMAND THE GOAL
LIKE MARY EARPS

It takes years of stopping shots and diving around in the mud to become a top keeper like Mary, but if you master the basics, you'll make more saves that you let in goals. Remember, NO goalkeeper can prevent every goal so try to bounce back quickly if you're beaten.

STEP 1: Invest in a pair of good quality padded gloves to avoid injuries from stinging shots.

STEP 2: When a shot heads your way, make sure that your set position is correct – plant your feet shoulder-width apart.

STEP 3: Keep your hands out ready, just above your waist – try imagining you're holding an invisible beach ball!

STEP 4: To catch a ball correctly that's heading towards your chest and above, you'll need to get your body behind the ball, creating a W-shape with your hands together. Below the waist, use the cup technique – clutch the ball tightly against your body to smother the shot.

STEP 5: Fingertip saves can look spectacular. When trying this save, use the fingers and top of the palm to direct the ball up and over the bar. Shuffle sideways in the direction of the shot, then push up from your legs to generate the power needed to explode towards the ball.

STEP 6: For any shots directed low into the corners, you'll need to get your body down to the ground quickly and lead with your hands. From your set position, throw the leg that is closest to the ball inwards and drop down to make the save. Keep your hands close together as you meet the ball and make the catch using a W-shape.

STEP 7: For shots that are hit hard and low towards your feet, you won't have time to make a full dive. Instead, use a foot save to make a strong contact with the ball and block the effort on goal. Check out Mary's fantastic stop in the Women's Euro 2022 semi-final for inspiration.